Hoodwinked II

Property Rights - Historical Perspective

ISBN: 978-1-7330672-2-5   [Paperback Edition]

Please visit *hoodwinked.net* for video versions of this manuscript.
Printed and bound in The United States of America.

Published by LittleHouse Enterprises Inc.

HOODWINKED II

The Illegal Taxation of Private American Homes

Vol. II
Property Rights - Historical Perspective

*The Arc of Land of Ownership
Rights from Old England to 1620 Plymouth,
to the American Revolution, to Modern Times*

J.A. PATRINA

Hoodwinked

Please visit HOODWINKED.NET
for video versions of this manuscript

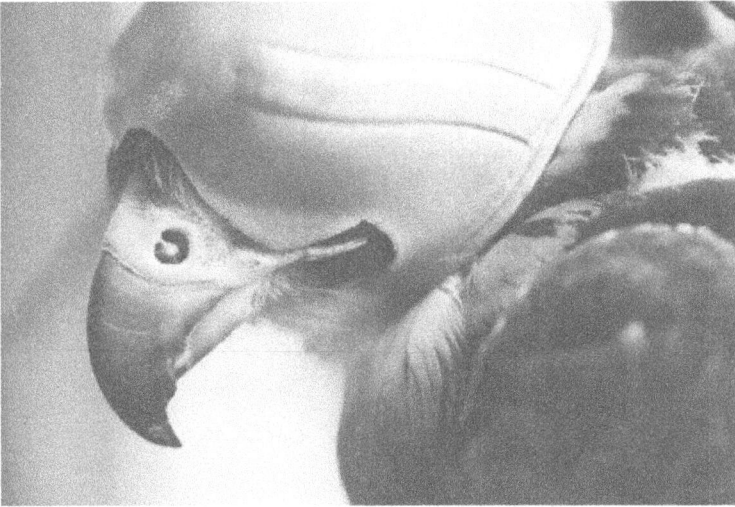

To be hoodwinked is to be deceived. The term actually derives from the practice of placing a hood over the head of a **falcon** in the Middle Ages when engaged in the **sport** of falconry. This practice **tricked** the falcon into believing it was nighttime, thus calming the bird so that one could recover the **prey** from the bird's talons - **Urban Dictionary**

Thomas Jefferson wrote,

"Educate and inform the whole mass of the people...
They are the only sure reliance for the preservation of our liberty."

There are Three (3) "Hoodwinked" books authored by Joe Patrina, the first constitutionally oriented, the second historically oriented, the third personally oriented.

Within these separate orientations, the books explore the natural and constitutional rights to private property held by all American citizens. This book, *Volume II – The Arc of Property Rights*, explains the foundation right to property that underpins the American legal system, and refers back to pre-revolution and even biblical references. Volume II also explains the assault on property by the socialist left in the modern era.

- *Hoodwinked Volume I – Constitutional Issues*
- *Hoodwinked Volume II – Historical Perspective*
  The Arc of Land Ownership Rights from Old England to 1620 Plymouth, to the American Revolution, to Modern Times
- *Hoodwinked Volume III – Town Hall – The Debasing of America*

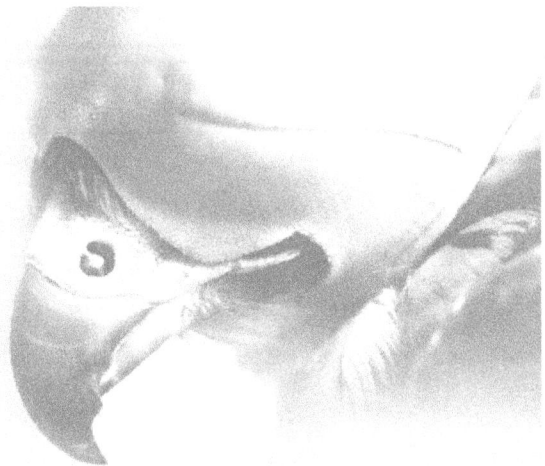

Author's Note

Home taxation is America's silent crisis. Without constitutional standing, municipalities use liens, foreclosure and wanton taking to inti-midate homeowners into paying any monies demanded. This unchallenged abuse of power tramples our *natural rights to life, liberty, and property,* and it completely abandons *due process,* the firewall protecting the individual against government overreach.

The **Hoodwinked** project came about in stages:

- It began when I protested local mill rates and pondered: *Does municipal budget voting actually sanction home taxation?*

- Next I met two Connecticut citizens suing the town over *"tax liens issued without due process."* In this case, a 1793 legislative grant asserting *absolute* rights to property is trampled upon by a conflicting 1875 lien statute. Towns incorrectly use the lien authority intended for commercial properties to *encumber* all of the so-called *absolutely owned* private citizen homes in Connecticut.

- Overall, I felt something deeply wrong, not just a state statute being abused wrong – a *Constitutional* wrong – and began to look into:

English Common Law; the Magna Carta; the John Locke Treatises on Government; Connecticut Colonial History; the Federalist Papers; the Declaration of Independence; the U.S. Constitution; the Bill of Rights; and many other writings – plus Supreme Court case law.

- My research found *no laws anywhere that give Federal, State, or Municipal governments free reign to tax private property.*

- Research, though, brought focus back to America's unique *Law of the Land.* The government is not in charge of everything! We were founded for government to protect our natural rights, not for government to undermine them! The *U.S. Constitution* prohibits government from chiseling wealth and liberty away from citizens. *Due process' very purpose safeguards property owners from their own government.*

And once so enlightened by my research, I next pondered: *Given our constitutional protections, how can municipal corporations invoice homeowners for taxes or for anything without having standard contracts that bind the homeowner to the municipality?* In other words, how do municipalities enjoy a claim on our properties, properties they are neither under contract with nor own, *while we, the home owners, sit powerless?*

Clearly, constitutional *due process* has been left behind, and Municipalities are now operating under an appearance (color) of law to confuse and intimidate citizens, thereby having their way with us.

Yet though property taxation lacks constitutional authority, some wring hands, mention *fairness,* and ask - *How, then, do we pay for the roads everyone drives on?* - not realizing that in-town annual road maintenance costs no more than a few hundred dollars per household.

Here is a quote from William Blackstone, the 1700's authority on English Common Law, and it illustrates the legal thinking during the Revolutionary period:

So great is the regard of the law for private property, that it will not authorize the least violation of it; no, not even for the general good of the whole community.

Personally, I would gladly pay for the few services the town provides. But … to have a municipal corporation - without agreement - bleed money from me by threatening a tax sale, followed by a sheriff with police backup knocking at my door, ready to drag me away … then the American in me says "no". Overall, we simply cannot allow modern, entrenched municipal budgets to derail our foundation laws; this practice is illegal. But what to do?

The *Hoodwinked* research has reached the point where professional constitutional experts can carry the case forward. An academic organization interested in American property rights is sought, one able to frame the constitutional case for presentation to the DOJ. The DOJ then challenges the State, navigates the court process and achieves what's known as *certiorari* (acceptance of the case) by the U.S. Supreme Court. If required, a property parcel (my house) already encumbered with a tax lien will be made available to anchor the case.

Hoodwinked, therefore, is not a protest or attempt to win hearts; it is not a debate about modern Democrats or Republicans, nor a debate about a biased media or activist judges, nor a debate about any of the other political bantering's burning up oxygen these days; it is a legally-based line of attack using strict Common, State and

U.S. Constitutional law to reverse the *illegal taxation of private American homes* paradigm – a severe violation of law and of our national origins. Please dig in, and thank you for getting involved.

Joe Patrina

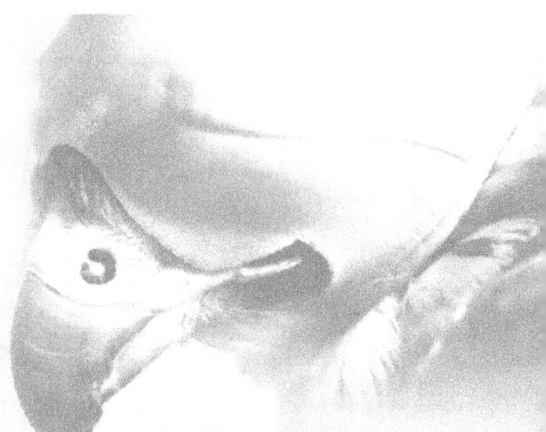

Bibliography & Research Topics

- The Bible – 1,800 BC
- The Magna Carta – 1215
- William Bradford History of Plymouth – 1620s
- Connecticut River Colony Constitution – 1630s
- Charles II Connecticut Charter – 1662
- The Glorious Revolution – 1688
- John Lock's Two Treatises of Government – 1688
- French/English Wars 1702 - 1765
- Montesquieu's Spirit of the Laws - 1748
- Virginia Militia – 1750's
- Rousseau's Social Contract - 1762
- War taxation 1770's
- Quartering & Writs of Assistance - 1770's
- "Common Sense" by Thomas Paine - 1776
- The Declaration of Independence - 1776
- The Treaty of Paris – 1781
- Society of the Cincinnati Historical Texts - 1780's
- The Federalist Papers – 1780s
- The U.S. Constitution – 1788
- The Bill of Rights – 1791
- The Rights of Man by Thomas Paine - 1791
- Ct 47-1 Land Rights – 1793

- The Unconstitutionality of Slavery –Lysander Spooner, 1845
- Bastiat's, The Law, 1850
- History of Connecticut, Vol I&II, Hollister - 1850
- Following 47-1 to 1865,
- "Allodial" Eliminated in 1865
- Tax Lien of 1875
- Government Schools Introduced
- Connecticut Constitution of 1965
- Winston Churchill's History of the English Speaking Peoples
- Churchill's Trial – Larry P. Arnn
- The Pat McCue/John Barney Case Law
- Due Process Case Law – U.S. Supreme Court
- Abortion Rights Case Law – Supreme Court
- Black's Law Dictionary
- Blackstone's Commentaries on Common Law

Contents

You have enemies? Good.
That means you've stood up for something,
something in your life.

— **Winston Churchill**

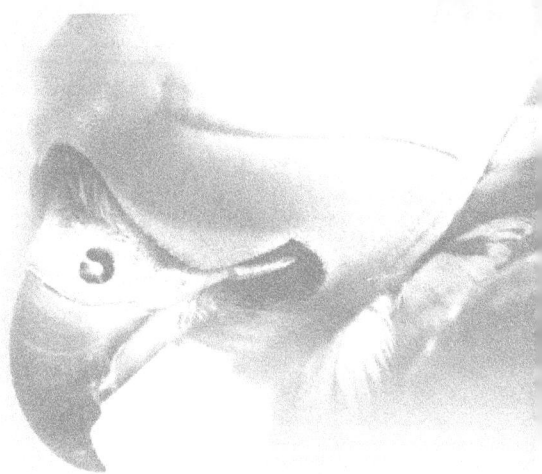

Chapter 1

America's Law of the Land

HOODWINKED asserts that U.S. Constitutional and state laws, as well as Common Law, all prohibit municipalities from taxing homeowners. As this book will prove, personal property tax, tax liens on homes, and property confiscation run illegal at many levels.

HOODWINKED describes how, without legal standing, municipalities use fear-of-confiscation to coerce citizens into voluntary abandonment of their *absolute, no-strings-attached* rights to property, substituting *limited, conditional* rights tied to imposed taxation and code strings. One no longer owns one's house *absolutely.* Instead, to keep your house, one must fulfill every tax and code *condition* demanded by the authorities.

HOODWINKED re-discovers one's *natural rights* to Life, Liberty and Property as affirmed by the Founders, protecting us from government overreach. To be valid, all laws must pass the Due Process of the Law of the Land test to assure that one's *natural rights* have not been tread upon. Property taxation clearly fails this test, trampling our "no strings attached" property rights at their very core.

HOODWINKED *further* describes how Due Process shields property owners from mob-rule voting, and from errant lawmakers, governors, and judges who cross the government authority line. Due Process barriers extend across many classes of property including homes (as examined in this document), but also to bank accounts, investment accounts, 401 K's, cars, boats, planes, inventions, one's own body and one's opinions, speech, and beliefs.

In America, all classes of property are considered absolutely owned, not subject to taxation, confiscation, or compromise by the government without compensation to the owner. Our Founding Fathers baked these ancient "natural" rights to property into the U.S. Constitution, with specific expressions of rights echoed in the statutes of each state, my state being Connecticut. Property taxation, as of yet unchallenged, is not "settled law", as advocates claim; it is instead "against the law".

Natural Law

The rights examined herein came out of English Common Law. English-speaking countries use a system of Common Laws that evolved over the ages, and are largely based on consensus and precedent. Conversely, Civil Law systems—think Russia—are largely based on a Code of Law written by the government, dictated to the people. France, for example, still operates off of the Napoleonic Code written by their famous dictator. From the English system comes the idea of Natural Law

and Natural Rights, things sitting above government, not decreed by government.

Natural rights—which have existed all along within American tradition—stand prior to any government, and sit within their own "timeless" realm. Back in 1215, the Magna Carta officially sanctioned "human rights from birth" through the *Due Process of the Law of the Land* test. Magna Carta enshrined the principle that the king had to act within the rule of law, not making un-authorized dictates up, violating Natural Law. Even today, newly enacted American laws, to be constitutional, must not impinge one's natural rights to Life, Liberty, and Property.

The above is not a fairy tale. In the U.S. Constitution, *Procedural* and *Substantive* Due Process provisions (described later) prohibit legislatures from enacting laws that limit one's general, natural rights. Listen ...

The Legislative has no right to absolute, arbitrary power over the lives and fortunes of the people.—**Samuel Adams, (1772)**

* * *

It is, in some sense, the case of every man among us who has property of which he may be stripped. For the question is simply this, 'Shall our State Legislatures be allowed to take that which is not their own, and apply it to such ends and purposes as they in their discretion shall see fit? Every citizen shall hold his life, liberty, and property under the protection of the general rules which govern society. Everything which may pass under the form of an enactment is not therefore to be considered the law of the land.—**Daniel Webster, 1818, Supreme Court, Dartmouth College Case**

What is this LAW OF THE LAND?

It is the collection of traditions, customs, statutes, usages, and laws of a country that apply to everyone, including the government. **Black's Law Dictionary.**

The natural, organically formed *Law of the Land*, effectively exists as the unwritten constitution of every nation. In America, the Law of the Land comprises the living principles followed in early America up to this day. And under America's natural law, no one ever authorized government to chip wealth or liberty away from the people through property assaults of any kind.

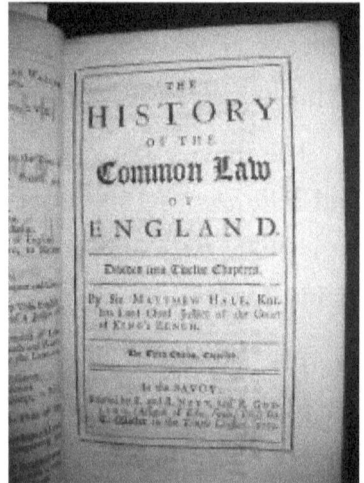

To achieve validity, written law—constitutional amendments, state statutes, town votes and ordinances—must conform *first* to the Law of the Land which protects the individual's natural rights. Natural rights, given to mankind "by God" at birth (or sooner), cannot be altered by legislation, property tax liens, or by town budget votes. Listen …

Due process of law does not mean merely according to the will of the Legislature, or the will of some judicial or quasi-judicial body upon whom it may confer authority. It means according to the law of the land, including constitutional limitations.—**Ekern v. McGovern, 1913**.

* * *

His rights existed by the law of the land long antecedent to the organization of the State.—**Hale v. Henkel, 1906, Supreme Court.**

Obviously, others seeking to rein in government came before this writing; I merely reconnect long-forgotten dots. *The government is not in charge of everything.* The founders, determined to contain government's role, weaved "Due Process" carve outs into the U.S. Constitution, which prohibit government from making laws that erode one's *natural* rights. Due Process forms a firewall, to government's lawmaking scope.

More, besides due process property right protection at the Common Law and federal level—which alone should protect our homes from taxation—at the state level, one finds a Connecticut founding 1793 Connecticut *Property Rights Statute—General Statute # 47-1.*

What is the significance of this? Everything! Like the U.S. Constitution, the state's founding Property Statute grants *absolute* rights to one's property. But municipal officials ignore this, and instead to assert their authority, quote the state's tax code which describes how to place liens

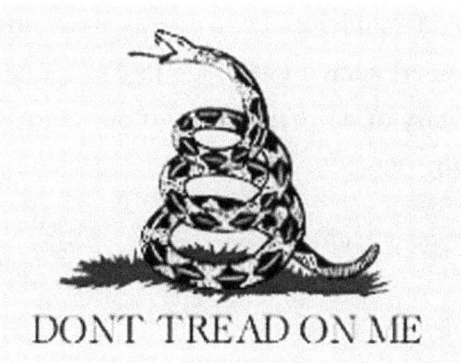

DONT TREAD ON ME

and take property. The statutes appear to sit in conflict. But once deconstructed, the two statutes apply to different situations. The absolute property right statute pertains to private property, the tax collection statutes to legally approved commercial properties. But today, incorrectly, commercial rules are being applied to private homes. This slight-of-hand situation is replicated by every State.

All States Are Protected—Though I did not examine the other 49 states coming on board during the next 200 years, all share the common "property is freedom" foundation of America. As such, all state laws must comport themselves to the *Due Process of the Law of the Land* clauses that protect Life, Liberty and Property as natural rights due to everyone.

Legal arguments for property taxes, tax liens or tax sales made by any state fail this standard, as these tax affronts implicitly undermine one's *absolute, natural rights* to Life, Liberty, and Property.

What is behind all this?

The ***HOODWINKED*** manuscript traces socialist forces maneuvering us away from both natural and written rights towards wanton state authority, and suggests a direct court challenge of state and municipal behavior as the starting point for reversal. But to assert such a challenge in court, one needs to understand the back story of property. We start our journey back in England, at Hastings in 1066.

Chapter 2

Hastings Battlefield & Allodialism

"No free man shall be seized or imprisoned, or stripped of his rights or possessions, or outlawed or exiled. Nor will we proceed with force against him except by the lawful judgement of his equals or by the law of the land. To no one will we sell, to no one deny or delay right or justice "—
Magna Carta.

I write about Hastings, not just to describe the famous battle between English Lords and the invading French Norman knights, but to relate how England's defeat, and the subsequent transfer of English land deeds to William the Conqueror, triggered an ongoing property right struggle between the Norman overlords and the subjugated English. The English would patiently fight back to regain the "natural rights" taken from them.

Most significantly, this English/Norman freedom struggle ultimately fed the ideals sitting behind the American Revolution.

The White Cliffs of Dover near where William the Conquer landed.

First let's review the situation leading up to Hastings from 400 A.D., when Roman Britain fell, to the year 1066 A.D., when the battle of Hastings took place

When Rome retreated from Britain around 406 A.D. various Germanic/Scandinavian tribes from across the North Sea—the

Engels, Saxons and Jutes—came in to fill the Roman vacuum. They took land from the indigenous Celtic peoples—called Britons. King Arthur, for example, was the Celtic who unified his people against this onslaught. By the way, England is called such as it was first known as **Eng**le **Land**, the Engle moniker eventually morphed into Angle, as in Anglo Saxon.

In 1066, the year of the Hastings battle, King Harold Godwinson, the English king, had only been on the throne for a year. His turn to be king was the result of 600 years of strife between Anglo Saxon noble lines who continually competed with each other. As it happened, King Harold's predecessor had no children, so when Harold took the crown other contenders, including his brother and his Norman cousin William, objected.

Over the course of 600 years leading up to Harold, the basic Anglo Saxon law of the land remained constant: commoner "Freemen" were truly free. They owned land absolutely without obligation to anyone. Their allegiance to the local chief was voluntary, usually based upon receiving either pay or favors from the chief whenever a war danger surfaced. But overall it was "hands off" each household's stuff.

No other society on earth followed this ideology. Humanity everywhere else was ruled by strong men who controlled everything. This unique relationship of the individual within society was at the heart of what it meant to be an Anglo Saxon. Rules preserving this tradition were built into what is called English Common Law. Even today, in United State courtrooms, anything not spelled out in the U.S. Constitution reverts back to English Common Law, grounded in the natural rights of individuals.

Owning land in this manner had been a tradition in the Anglo Saxon world since the old days, back in Germany and Denmark, way before these invaders sailed to England around 400 A.D.

Land title of this nature is called "allodial title". Allodial ownership is unfettered, outright and absolute. Allodial ownership supposes no obligation to any lord or government body.

For example, the English Lords who fought at Hastings each held estates with allodial titles. But upon defeat, and with swords at their necks, the individual English Lords each ceded their personal allodial estates to William the Conqueror, who now claimed allodial title, not just for a given estate, but for all of the major estates of England.

William never abolished the Common Law concept of allodial title, he fully embraced it, becoming the absolute owner of all England. But to govern, William needed the English Lords to operate their former domains. So William granted what are called Feudal deeds back to the various English Lords. This allowed the English back on their estates, so long as they respected William's Feudal terms, which meant staying in William's good graces, paying any tax demanded, and joining William's army upon notice. This imposed way of life was a deep fall from the allodial England long enjoyed by the Anglo Saxon world, making England, like the rest of Europe, suddenly Feudal, run by totalitarian overlords.

Let's look at the events of 1066, describing how all of this went down. The controversy of Harold becoming king led two foreigners to take aim on the weakened England. The first, the aforementioned William, Duke of Normandy and the second King Harald III the Swede, both plotting unaware of the other.

King Harold of England was unaware of the two gathering storms, busy at home dealing with other threats, such as from his own brother. King Harald III (left) struck first, landing his ships north in York, England.

When word of this reached London, King Harold called upon his English Lords and formed an army of, say, 5,000. It is said that King Harold's personal guard counted 500 men wielding double-blade battle axes.

This army marches to York and at the battle of Stamford Bridge slaughters the Swedish forces, killing the blond, seven-foot tall King Harald III in the process.

While recuperating in York, Harold learns that William of Normandy, who all along asserted some claim on the English crown, had just landed in the south, below Dover, near a village called Hastings.

English King Harold marches his whole army 200 miles from York back to London, enlists re-enforcements, and then quickly pivots towards Hastings, another 70 miles away. He confronts William in October.

The exact numbers present at the battle are unknown; modern estimates are around 10,000 for William and about 7,000 for Harold. The composition of the forces is clearer; the English army was composed almost entirely of infantry and had few archers, whereas only about half of the invading force was infantry, the rest split equally between cavalry and archers.

King Harold appears to have tried to surprise William, but scouts found his army and reported its arrival to William, who marched from Hastings to the battlefield to confront Harold. The battle lasted from about 9 am to dusk. Early efforts of the invaders to break the English battle lines had little effect; therefore, the Normans adopted the tactic of pretending to flee in panic and then turning on their pursuers.

King Harold's death—shot in the eye by an arrow—probably near the end of the battle, led to the retreat and defeat of most of his army—half died, all surrendered their estates. After further marching and some skirmishes, William was crowned as king on Christmas Day 1066.

To commemorate the event, William commissioned a 50-scene, 230-foot long tapestry depicting the battle. Miraculously, it survives to this day, housed in Bayeux Normandy.

William's "French" Normans who had just taken London, quickly go about consolidating their hold over the conquered English Lords. At the time, compared to the Normans, in many respects, the English were fairly backward, probably because England stood isolated from the rest of Europe.

(Wooden Hill Fort)

Besides lacking cavalry and archers, English "hill forts" were still primitive timber and earth constructs.

The Normans quickly built stone castles, with The Tower of London a good example of their masonry abilities. Soon the English nobles could not rebel even if so inclined.

Physical separation using castles was combined with language separation, as the Norman nobles would speak only French for many decades to come. William sent his most loyal knights throughout the realm, forming a web of castles holding back the English.

In this manner Feudal absolutism became the new law of the land, and as such, William's successors ruled with an iron fist. Once England was under control, the Normans expanded their web into Wales, Ireland and Scotland, planting Norman knights everywhere and using marriages with local nobles to smooth things over.

(Tower of London)

150 years later, this tight Feudal system was finally challenged due to the excesses of King John, brother of Richard the Lionhearted. John's cruelty and his wanton taxation practices (as in Robin Hood and the Sheriff of Nottingham), to fight his own family, caused even the lesser Norman nobles to organize, threatening John, getting him to sign The Magna Carta in 1215 A.D.

Amongst its many provisions, the Carta proclaims that government is not to impinge upon what are considered "natural rights". Things like random executions are no longer tolerated. Each person charged or engaged in dispute has the natural right to "due process".

The Magna Carta was the first *claw back* in favor of the individual against the enslavement of Feudalism, and five hundred years later Thomas Jefferson would include its premise into the Declaration of Independence, citing life, liberty and the pursuit of happiness as "natural rights" bestowed by the creator, not by the fickle benevolence of government.

One more thing deciphered by Jefferson includes his brilliant insight that since the various English nobles at Hastings had turned title over to William, that indeed the English King had allodial title to most of England, but in America, no such transfer of allodial title from the colonists to the King had ever taken place, nor had any conquest of America by the king occurred.

Hence the King's allodial claims in America was fraudulent, this becoming a key argument underpinning the American Revolution (Jefferson's writing on this point is presented later in the book). And once the Americans won the war with England, they went on to write a constitution that protected absolute, natural rights to property. What is more, government's job was to protect these natural rights at the town, state and federal levels—never to impinge or encumber them.

Much more on this later in the manuscript. Next we advance 600 years and learn how the HOODWINKED manuscript came about.

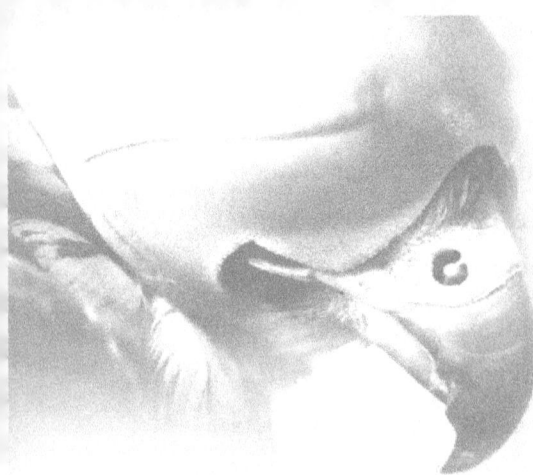

Chapter 3

Hoodwinked's Back Story

Land ownership in Connecticut has a long history:

It started with almost no rules within the 1620-era Puritan townships, where barter and lack of documentation meant no enforceable title claims.

The English King Charles II only established formal ownership parameters in 1662 through thew Connecticut Charter, by declaring himself the supreme owner.

In defeat, England signed the 1782 Treaty of Paris, ceding land title to the Americans as long as the Revolutionary War victors did not confiscate the properties of Americans loyal to the king.

By 1788, the American founders designed the U.S. Constitution, working from a deep conviction that freedom equates to absolute ownership of one's property—property comprising one's life, one's land and movable holdings, and the use of one's holdings. These are natural rights.

By 1793, the various legislatures of the 13 founding states, including Connecticut, etched the land right concepts of the U.S. Constitution into statute. Property cannot be encumbered.

Over the subsequent 200 years, advocates seeking monies to foster government school programs (and advance other agendas) cleverly injected murky land-right doubts into the minds of the citizenry, thus allowing illegal property taxation to take hold.

Today, homeowners have much deeper published rights than they realize. Over time, creeping forces have so stealthily obscured the inalienable nature of private property that *until now*, no one pursued or defended these forgotten rights. But they exist—right under our very noses.

How did this manuscript come to pass?

I started researching these topics a few years back, when I ran a one-man campaign to defeat the new town budget.

I designed signs making my anti-budget case, and placed them around town on friendly yards. The town took them down, as I had not first filed signed permission forms at town hall from the property owners, although the owners had gladly planted the signs. So, instead I hired some teens to hold the signs in front of the post office, at the shopping mall, and at the polling site.

My lesson soon came. Of the 9,000 households in town, and the 16,000 or so eligible voters, only 800 voted. The total town employee roster, including teachers, came to 1,000, and emails had gone out to these employees encouraging them to vote (for their self-interest). The budget easily passed, as it always will.

I could not believe that the town could demand even more money from me based upon this ridiculous vote. Then my mind traveled further. Even if everyone had voted, I could not believe voting constituted a justifiable basis to grab money from homeowners... so I dug deeper.

Research conducted by two friends of mine, *Pat McCue and John Barney* (more on these guys later) found no Connecticut statutes stating that towns had taxing authority over people's houses.

I challenged the local tax collector about this, who said a statute indeed existed, Connecticut General Statutes Section 12-171-to-174, authorizing tax liens. McCue and Barney previously explained this to me, so I just listened, amazed at the tax collector's nonchalant attitude toward confiscating people's homes with or without judicial oversight.

CT 12-171-to-174 series cites the town's power to place a tax lien on properties with the ability to confiscate and sell the property if needed: not an authority to tax, but a "stand alone" lien procedure (one that will shortly present itself as unconstitutional at Common Law, state and federal levels).

So, it dawned on me, the town can place a lien to collect unpaid taxes without first having taxation powers, making the liens pure extortion! What kind of slight-of-hand is this?

McCue and Barney had dug into this at the Connecticut Law Library in Hartford, where all of Connecticut's statute books going back to and before the Revolution sit. They said the lien statute passed in 1875, but that it only applied to commercial property taxation.

But they also said that a statute, written in 1793, gave private non-commercial property owners "absolute," no-strings-attached ownership, protecting the owner from encumbrances such as taxation, liens, and code. This statute changed slightly over time, but still stood in the books as CGS 47-1.

So, not only did towns lack taxation authority, but, by granting absolute title to homeowners in 1793, CGS 47-1 strictly prohibited government meddling with extortion-like tax liens or any other encumbrance device, period! How then, do towns lien homes and legally confiscate them?

Legally they cannot. As outlined, Connecticut's 1875 tax lien code was never intended for *illegal taxation* of homes; it was written for *legal taxation* of commercial property. Municipalities ignore the distinction, and no one challenges them.

And anyway, what kind of a lien are they talking about?

Liens come into play when two parties have *an agreement* and one party does not hold up their end of the bargain. The harmed party applies for a court lien from a judge, freezing the property in question, thereby putting pressure on the errant counterparty to come to resolution.

For example: a plumber goes unpaid, with his pipes and labor expenses trapped in his customer's building. The plumber appeals to a judge, presents the work order agreement and evidence of a completed job, and so the judge grants the lien. The lien puts anyone else wanting to do business with the errant building owner on notice that the property does not stand free and clear. The owner needs to settle, or appear in court.

In the town's property tax situation, the town and the private-citizen homeowners *never struck any agreement* and hence no agreement exists to break. Further, the town never went to court with due process to obtain a judicial lien.

The town simply made the lien up on its own, having no broken agreement with the homeowner to base the lien upon and no due process interaction with the court to get the lien approved; they simply issued it *unilaterally*—something called "a non-judicial take."

ARE YOU READING THIS? Yes, it's as bad as you think: an outright confidence hustler's trick perpetrated on a huge scale, something I call *"National Grifting"*!

OK, the whole tax-lien thing smells illegal, likely criminal under Color of Law (abuse of power) due to its extortion tactic, but what does the Ct 1793 property rights statute say to further define the extent of the town's extortionist behavior?

The Ct 1793 property statute states that prior to the Revolution, property owners were beholden to the king, who had "allodial" title to all property. "Allodial" means that the king's right to use, bequeath, or take back property comes from God and cannot be challenged by man. We will examine the word "allodial" in depth later in this manuscript, and though not a word used in modern times, the concept of "allodialism" (standing above government) stood as a centerpiece of the founders in designing American law.

The 1793 statute goes on to say that the same claim of allodial title once enjoyed by the king… now belongs to owners of property in Connecticut.

Moreover, the 1793 statute says that the legal wording of the new statute replaces the old declaration of property rights stated in the Charles II Charter of 1662. We will analyze the statute's wording later, but generally speaking, the words give *absolute control* to the homeowners, not *conditional control* based upon, say, a tax bill paid in full.

After reading Connecticut laws referring back to charters issued in 1662, I decided to trace private property aspirations from the times of the 400 A.D. Anglo Saxon invasion of Britain to the

1600s Native American and Pilgrim era in the New World, up to the creation of Connecticut's 1793 statute… and so I did. From this I drew a bead on America's *Law of the Land*—just outlined in chapter I, and further described at the end of the book.

I subsequently traced the legal maneuvering of property rights from 1793 through the 1800s and 1900s to current time, using the research of McCue and Barney, and by reading U.S. Supreme Court findings. From this I discovered why the Connecticut lien statute as applied to private homes is unconstitutional at both state (*a statute illegally applied*) and federal (*due process violation*) levels.

This manuscript covers the research carried out across those two respective historical periods—ancient and modern. And as the reader will discover, ancient law and our modern U.S. Constitution both fundamentally guarantee the rights expressed in the 1793 Connecticut property statute.

Over the course of this writing, the reader will follow the arc of property rights in America, whereby:

1. Before 1793, the king fraudulently claimed "allodial" title to American property; you used land only by ful-

filling the King's conditions;

2. In the Post-Revolutionary period up to the Civil War individuals truly owned their property with "allodial" absolute rights as intended by the founders; and

3. During the slide into modern times, State Legislatures—without changing Common Law, the U.S. Constitution or state statutes—slowly clawed control away from homeowners (just as in the era of kings), tricking homeowners with the obligation to pay taxes and fulfill other conditions such as obeying code and zoning dictates, if they wanted to continue to "own" their property.

Rather than citizens living with the government at our service—once again we became subjects and vassals of an imagined higher power. We were hoodwinked!

Manuscript Organization

To understand American property rights, one needs to follow history from old English Common Law through to the American Revolution and the design of America's Constitution, finally digging down to the state statute level.

U.S. Constitutional arguments are covered in detail in *Hoodwinked—Volume I—Constitutional Issues*. This book presents a historical framework on how Federal and State protections were formulated and then abused.

We will achieve this historical analysis as follows:

1. In a **Statutory context**, by examining the language of Connecticut's 1793 property rights statute (CGS 47-1) describing our absolute rights to property: presented in *Chapter 4—Connecticut General Statute 47-1*.

2. In a **Connecticut historical context**, by examining the aspirations of those state representatives who assembled said language, allowing one to gauge the mindset of the people of that time: presented in *Chapter 5—Connecticut's Historical Context*.

3. Most importantly, in a **national context**, by peering into the philosophies of the founders, who designed the government to protect citizen properties from government encumbrance: presented in *Chapter 6—Founding Principals*.

4. In a **political context**, by tracing the series of stealth moves, such as the sinister 1875 lien statute that slowly entrapped citizens into paying property taxes: presented in *Chapter 7—Legalized Plunder*.

5. In a **judicial context**, by outlining the case law of McCue and Barney, and how it was dismissed out of hand in court: presented in *Chapter 8—Connecticut Yankees*.

6. In a **legal history context**, a 4,000-year chronology of property rights, including Supreme Court cases: presented in *Chapter 9—English and American Case Law.*

7. In a **"what to do" context,** presented in *Chapter 10—Fighting for our Law of the Land.*

8. In a **recap context**, presented as: *Appendix A—Socialist Checklist, Appendix B—Natural Rights, Appendix C—Indirect and Direct Taxation, and Appendix D—Famous Socialists.*

Also...

One of the reasons our property rights remain successfully hidden is all the slow-moving, difficult-to-track moving parts of the story. We cannot keep up, so we become hoodwinked, and go along with what we are told. It took years for the author to sort out the contents of this document, so please bear with the detail.

Next up, a look at CGS Statute 47-1, defining what is meant by *absolute* property rights in my state of Connecticut.

Here: Roger Sherman of Connecticut — one of the authors of CGS 47-1— and the only person to sign all four great state papers of the U.S., including: The Continental Association (a 1774 trade boycott with England), The Declaration of Independence, the Articles of Confederation and The U.S. Constitution.

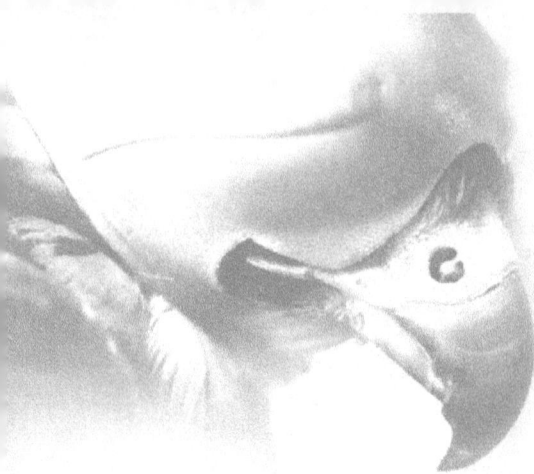

Chapter 4

Connecticut General Statutes Section 47-1

Before moving up to the level of the U.S Constitution, we'll start by examining the legal language of Connecticut General Statutes Section 47-1, defining property rights in Connecticut.

The statutes of each state exist in books marked by the year the statutes were in effect. Each year's edition reflects added and/ or retired statutes, plus modified, ongoing statutes. Often, minor changes to existing statutes became law through a routine "up-or-down" legislative vote upon the entire edition, the details not scrutinized. This, you will see, happened with changes to CGS 47-1. Often legislative behavior does not take place above board, the detail wording of laws modified in stealth by a few men in the back office, the language approved *en masse*.

To follow the statutory history of CGS 47-1, you can read the Connecticut statute books, starting with the current period and going back in time to the first laws published by Connecticut after the Revolution.

Recall that the states ratified the U.S. Constitution in 1788, the Bill of Rights shortly thereafter in 1791, and that …

... any subjects not assigned by the Constitution to the federal government remain for the individual states to decide upon, including aspects of one's rights to property, and ...

... anything not spelled out at either state or federal levels falls back upon old English Common Law (much more on English Common Law later), especially in areas of due process pertaining to property.

After the Revolution, internally, Connecticut continued to operate under the old Charles II Charter of 1662 (described next in *Chapter 5—Connecticut Historical Context*), moving to a state constitution only in 1818.

Following the procedural rules of the old charter, the post-revolution Connecticut state assembly began the process of crafting new laws consistent with the people's independence from the British monarch.

One of these, formulated in 1793, defined one's rights in owning property, as presented below. This statute appears in the subsequent editions of Connecticut law to this day. Over time, it received various filing numbers, and today sits as Connecticut General Statutes Section 47-1. As mentioned, lawmakers modified some of the original language, but the key right of what we call "absolute ownership" remains the statute's centerpiece, as follows:

ACTS and LAWS

Made and passed by the General Court or Assembly of the State of Connecticut, in America, holden at New-Haven, (in said State) on the second Thursday of October, Anno Domini 1793.

An Act declaring the Tenure of Lands in this State.

Whereas, *by the Charter of Charles II, the Lands in the then Coloney of Connecticut, were holden of the King of England, by the Tenure of Free and Common Socage, and by the establishment of the Independence of the United States, the citizens of this State became vested with an allodial Title to their Lands.*

BE it therefore declared by the Governor and Council, and House of Representatives, in General Court assembled, that every Proprietor in fee simple of Lands, has an absolute and direct dominion, and property in the same. *Tenure of Land*

These are not typo's. The above appears as written back in 1793.

As we will revisit in the next chapters, the central issue regarding property rights remains the extent of one's rights. Let's get started by understanding the "extent" of one's rights... what does that really mean?

For example, you might lease a plot of land from a neighbor to grow corn, with the lease specifying growing corn your sole right to the property, and only for one summer. You cannot build a house, chop down trees, remove stones from the leased property, or do anything without written consent besides growing corn.

You have very *limited* property rights in this case.

The opposite case is *absolute* rights, meaning you can do what you want with the property with no preconditions—such as paying an annual tax—and no encumbrances—such as getting permission from zoning for changes you envision for your house.

The framers of the 1793 statute went out of their way to leave no doubt as to the extent of one's rights to privately owned property— the rights are absolute. Here are the *Black's Law* legal definitions to the words:

So cage	The hereditary system of the feudal Kings to hold all lands for themselves and to grant others only the use of lands. "So cage" is being retired by the statute.
Vested	Meaning that new rights being assigned are fixed, providing complete ownership, not contingent or subject to be defeated by condition or precedent.
Allodial	Not holden of any lord or superior; owned without vassalage or fealty (faithfulness). Held by absolute ownership, without recognizing any superior to whom any duty is due on account thereof. Meaning these new rights are not the gift of the government but sit above government, not able to be taken.
Fee simple of Lands	The way land was owned beneath the King, meaning those who previously owned their land under a "fee simple" arrangement before the Revolution are now candidates for the new set of rights.
Absolute	Unconditional, without any exception, restriction, qualification, or limitation. The new rights.
Direct	not stopping. The new rights.
Dominion	Perfect control in one's right to property. The new rights.
Tenure	Permanent rights of property ownership. The time frame of the new rights.

Reread the statute and definitions to be sure, and then consider: do I own my house in this manner?

Mind you, though absolute rights in Connecticut obviously means unlimited, this does not mean these rights are respected and routinely enforced as so.

Conversely, Connecticut courts seem unaware of absolute rights, or if aware, they turn a blind eye to these rights. After all, in affirming absolute rights, *property taxation* would be overturned, as it places a condition on the extent of ownership. You own the property only so long as you pay the taxes, otherwise the government seizes and sells the property. This is not "absolute" ownership as provided by the law.

Such a ruling affirming "absolute" rights would end the current tax collection methodology... a political conundrum for the judges. We will look at fixing this tax conundrum in *Appendix C – Direct and Indirect Taxation.* For now, let's stay focused on how it currently works.

Banks

I sincerely believe... that banking establishments are more dangerous than standing armies.—**Jefferson**

Conveyance of title—between a seller and a buyer—can be written with or without strings attached. If the seller agrees to forgo any and all rights to the buyer, the buyer receives the status of "absolute rights" to the title, and should be protected by the 1793 statute.

If, however, the buyer pays for the property using a bank loan, the bank may insist that the buyer agrees to pay all property taxes demanded by the municipality. The deed includes this freely agreed-upon compliance and the new owner willingly files it at town hall.

The bank wants no slip-ups over the course of the loan's term, such as unpaid taxes, at which point the town could get first dibs on selling the property from under the bank, grabbing its tax money, leaving what's left to the bank. The bank does not commit this kind of financial suicide, so...

To get the loan, one cedes *absolute* rights and accepts *limited* rights—a loan based upon paying taxes. One accepts a *consensual lien* to get the loan.

Moreover, the bank pays the taxes each month from the lump sum you shell out to the bank, covering tax, insurance, interest, and principal components. If you cannot pay, the bank is the first to know, and they control the liquidation process, assuming full title, paying the tax and insurance themselves until a suitable buyer comes along.

In writing a new deed involving a bank loan, language on the deed names the title holder obliged to pay taxes, such as: *The title holder agrees to have the property placed on the grand list and pay all taxes, etc.*

But if a buyer can swing a loan with no strings attached, or the buyer owns property outright, that buyer moves up to the *absolute rights* classification. In doing so, the deed on file should be explicit, saying something as follows:

The title holder owns the property free and clear and has no contractual obligation to the town of XXX...

Now that the buyer has ditched the bank, this alternative deed language makes clear that ownership is not inadvertently entwined in an implied contractual agreement with the municipality. If under contract with the municipality, even by mistake, the municipality retains the right to go to court and seek a lien if you do not fulfill your "tax promise" agreement.

This partnership between banks and tax authorities, needs spelling out. By working symbiotically, each gets what it wants: banks get tight control over their customers and the mortgaged properties, earning interest at lower risk levels, and the municipality gets tax monies dropped at their doorstep. And, to seduce you into buying expensive homes, you can deduct both the property taxes and interest expenses. The bank and the town have buried their hooks deep, and you feel like you are doing great.

As we will see in *Chapter 7—Legalized Plunder*, municipalities get away with ignoring CGS 47-1 altogether, not just in these gray areas... worse, they ignore the due process clauses within the U.S. Constitution.

"The devil!" you say.

OK, the municipality breaks the law and no one cares, though technically laws protecting the individual stand intact and clear. What to do?

A Strict Matter of Law—Without Disputed Facts to Muddy Things Up

And so I present the proposition of this manuscript: With the law so vivid, skillful attorneys could assemble effective litigation to confront *the financial damages of illegal taxes and bogus liens* perpetrated by towns, and shut down the willful *abuse of power tactics* used by the municipality to intimidate and bankrupt a private citizen minding their own business on their own private property.

But with the practice so entrenched, it sits beyond the possibility of a common citizen to take the whole machine on. In Chapter 8— Connecticut Yankees, we will find out what happens when a common citizen speaks up. This is why the Department of Justice needs to take up the case. At some point, with persistent legal representation by the DOJ controlling both the legal arguments and the procedural court tactics, fraudulent tax extortion by the states could be exposed and ended ... the way slavery was ended in 1865, leaving everyone to adjust to a new and proper human rights configuration. So, that is the goal, though I need a lot of help. This use of published legal protections stands a pivotal chance to deflate socialist forces and their quest to debase private property.

But the process comprises many moving parts, and so we cover many topics in this short manuscript: talking points to guard against attempts by the tax advocates to trip you up or push you off the path.

For example, looking ahead to *Chapter 7—Legalized Plunder*, we will confront the driver behind this fraud: the need to fund government schools. You'll learn that in 1965, Connecticut ratified a new constitution, making free education a right for all children. But the law never specified how to pay for it all, nor even defined what constitutes "free education."

Connecticut Article 8, Section 1 from 1965: *There shall always be free public elementary and secondary schools in the state. The general assembly shall implement this principle by appropriate legislation.*

This mushy directive for free education inspired open-ended appetites for greater and greater education expenditures. The financing of this landed illegally on the shoulders of private homeowners, who, by Due Process and the CT 47-1 "Absolute Rights" statute, cannot be so encumbered.

The state owns this law and its obligation—not you, not me—and the state's remedies include measures such as increased sales and income taxes—but not our houses.

My rights on all of this are clear, and so is my attitude: with absolute ownership, the homeowner stands independent of any superiors and free of any property right restrictions such as taxes and code.

Next up, in Chapter 5—Connecticut's Historical Context, the reader will be in very good company with individuals who struggled for liberty.

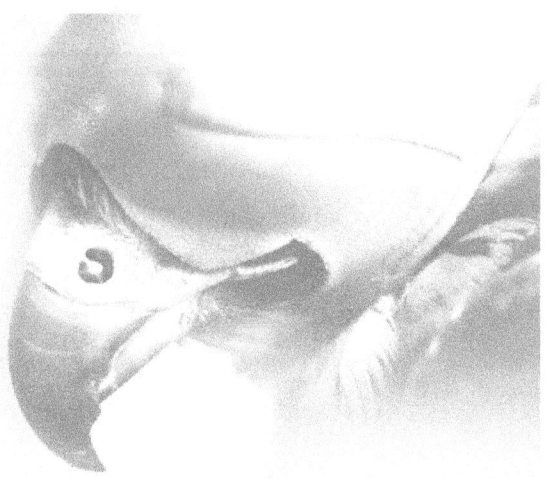

Chapter 5

Connecticut's Historical Context

We next examine why in 1793 the citizens of Connecticut came to demand absolute rights over their property.

Some say "We don't care what people in 1793 thought when they drafted their *property rights statute*; 1793 is irrelevant!"

As a tactic, pro-tax people shun historical precedence and concepts such as *natural rights* and *the Law of the Land*, preferring instead to invent law and tax obligations that suit their evolving agenda. But if you value the rule of law, you will appreciate reading what Connecticut's settlers experienced leading up to the 1793 passage of *"An Act Declaring the Tenure of Lands in this State"*, the people's definitive assertion regarding property rights.

To begin, once entering the realm of historical context, consider that the Connecticut people's intent in formulating law back in 1793 certainly differed from, for example, the intent of Georgia in drawing up Georgian state laws. One of the reasons the country chose state's rights as its constitutional bedrock, rather than centralized control (à la the Russia and China), stems from the vast differences in historical context from state to state: in America, context matters!

In Connecticut's specific case, starting from the first settlers and leading up to the 1793 property rights statute, our residents demonstrated a definitive thirst for both individual liberties, and, later, optimized rights involving private property. Hence a Connecticut-centric context remains paramount toward understanding the intent of present day CGS 47-1 within the law of the land.

So where do we start?

With Connecticut's settlers, those who migrated from Massachusetts up the Connecticut River in 1633, some 13 years after the Mayflower landed at Plymouth Rock. From 1633, we trace their steps to the Revolution.

The Separatists

Critical point: The Mayflower people who settled Plymouth and then entered Connecticut were *Separatists*, a subset of the "vanilla" Puritan movement taking place in England from the late 1500s to about 1640.

The "vanilla" Puritan movement sought to remold the Church of England toward more fundamental Christian practices. Puritans complained that the Church of England differed little from the Catholic Church it left under Henry VIII.

Puritans, in general, believed that the Bible existed as God's true law, and thus it provided a plan for living. But like Catholicism, The Church of England made access to God possible only within the confines of "church authority", a state-imposed religion.

Puritans wanted to strip away the cobwebs built by the Catholic Church throughout the previous 1500 years, still intact within the Church of England. Theirs was an attempt to "purify" England's church and their own lives via direct communion with God.

Separatists, in contrast, comprised a more radical Puritan sect who had fully given up trying to reform the Church of England. In their eyes, the only course of action came down to total separation from society. While holding religious freedom at center, Separatists sought separation in every aspect of life: culture, morality, and economy.

The Mayflower Separatists, led by William Bradford and Myles Standish, who first moved from England to Holland for religious freedom before coming to America, wanted control over their economy and did not want their children contaminated by the ways of the English or the Dutch. A separatist believed he or she must shield all aspects of running life from wanton authority and unwanted influences.

And so, a decade later, these Mayflower Separatists migrated west from Cape Cod to become Connecticut's first settlers, founding the Connecticut River Colony in 1633, made up of the Windsor, Hartford, and Wethersfield townships. They apparently feared little, so long as freedom rang—loudly, with hundreds of them willing to survive harsh winters and Indian treachery.

A second group of Connecticut settlers came out of Boston's Massachusetts Bay Colony, a detached colony from Plymouth Colony.

Connecticut Pilgrims

Massachusetts Bay, settled in 1630 (10 years after Plymouth in 1620),
began with the arrival of 16 boats filled with English Puritans,
led by John Winthrop.

Whereas Plymouth leaders William Bradford and Myles Standish espoused separatism, Massachusetts Bay's leader, John Winthrop, preached moderate Puritanism, believing the Church of England could still be fixed. Winthrop, author of *The Shining City on the Hill* sermon, simply wanted to set an example for England to follow—our first elitist!

Though 10 years behind Plymouth, some Boston residents got wind of the settling activities down in Connecticut, but the elitism of Winthrop's Boston magistrates dictated that these residents would stay put in the yet-to-be-nicknamed "Bay State."

Regardless, some defiant Boston *wanderlust* types eventually moved to Connecticut, so that overall, Connecticut's genetic stock gravitated to those Englishmen craving real freedom. This core stock of fiercely independent people would multiply almost exponentially—many families having 10 children—and would remain undiluted into the 1800s, when Irish, Italian, Polish, French-Canadian, Jewish, Black, and Latino bloodlines joined.

These founding English families comprised the Connecticut Yankees.

The Absence of Land Rights Amongst Both Indian and Pilgrim Peoples

Various Indian tribes lived in Connecticut in those days, primarily along the coast and river valleys, with a population of 30,000 set against an English population of a mere 500. The vast area north of where Connecticut, New York, and Massachusetts convened stood uninhabited, used only by the tribes to hunt during the warmer weather.

The Native Americans did not own land. Instead, they moved through territories to glean natural resources, with tribes fighting each other when things got tight.

The English, therefore, did not receive title from the Indians when holding land. The English merely occupied the land as did the Indians, conflicts avoided via gifts and treaties, not land rights. The English adopted the Indian ways of loose land ownership.

More, these Separatist settlers themselves moved from temporary homesteads to new virgin land whenever it suited them, especially if power structures in a given congregation made some families feel slighted, thus moving on to establish new freedom.

Title simply did not exist among any of the players.

Uncas—The Mohegan Chief

In the Native American world, the squaws (females) did all of the real work, including farming; the males hunted and fought. Indeed, Native Americans sat amused watching Englishmen doing women's work. The Indians appreciated English guns, though, yet no evidence proved the English would use the guns upon their Indian neighbors. Instead, Indians pined for guns to go after other Indians to settle grudges.

Enter, stage right, Uncas, sachem of the Mohegan tribe, in central Connecticut on the river, approximately today's Middletown. Uncas lived almost 100 years, from 1588 to 1683 as perhaps the most skillful politician in New England during the colonial period, able to make the English do his bidding.

How so?

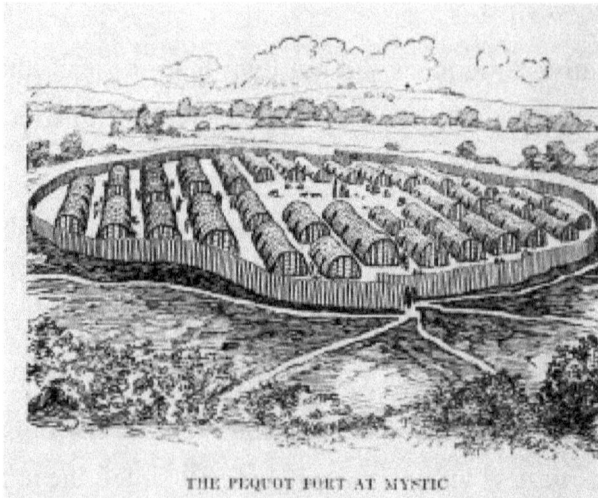

THE PEQUOT FORT AT MYSTIC

The Pequot Fort

Uncas hated the Pequot's, a sizable Indian nation living fortified further east on the Mystic river. First, he thoroughly convinced the English to trust his word. In 1637 he claimed the Pequot's conspiring to attack the fledgling English townships along the Connecticut river. Together, Uncas and the English defeat the Pequot's, and the survivors—the females—became part of the Mohegan Nation. As a further reward, in 1638, the Mohegan's officially become part of the Connecticut River Colony.

Next, a similar move by Uncas in 1640 folded the Hammonassett's into his tribe. Finally, in 1642, Uncas and the English wiped out the Narragansett's along the current Rhode Island border, with Uncas's brother tomahawking the captured Narragansett chief.

Lovely times abound, and to be sure, property rights did not exist, nor did the rule of law. Instead, pure unprotected survival proclaims Connecticut's way: definitely an unfettered form of freedom.

The Connecticut Colony Constitution

By 1639, the people within the Connecticut River Colony, living in an extremely autonomous fashion even among themselves, not beholden to Plymouth or Boston, with no relationship whatsoever with Mother England or the Crown... decided to form a country.

The starting point? Draw up the first constitution ever written by free men in the history of mankind. They called it *The Fundamental Orders of 1639*. Its first sentence (and it's a long one) follows:

For as much as it hath pleased Almighty God by the wise disposition of his divine providence so to order and dispose of things that we the Inhabitants and Residents of Windsor, Hartford and Wethersfield are now cohabiting and dwelling in and upon the River of Connectecotte and the lands thereunto adjoining; and well knowing where a people are gathered together the word of God requires that to maintain the peace and union of such a people there should be an orderly and decent Government established according to God, to order and dispose of the affairs of the people at all seasons as occasion shall require; do therefore associate and conjoin ourselves to be as one Public State or Commonwealth; and do for ourselves and our successors and such as shall be adjoined to us at any time hereafter, enter into Combination and Confederation together, to maintain and preserve the liberty and purity of the Gospel of our Lord Jesus which we now profess, as also, the discipline of the Churches, which according to the truth of the said Gospel is now practiced amongst us; as also in our civil affairs to be guided and governed according to such Laws, Rules, Orders and Decrees as shall be made, ordered, and decreed as followeth:

Quite a sentence! There are 11 provisions, with #11 mentioning taxes:

It is Ordered, sentenced, and decreed, that when any General Court upon the occasions of the Commonwealth have agreed upon any sum, or sums of money to be levied upon the several Towns within this Jurisdiction, that a committee be chosen to set out and appoint what shall be the proportion of every Town to pay of the said levy, provided the committee be made up of an equal number out of each Town.

Basically, if the territory required taxes to, say, fight Indians, then everyone needed to chip in on equal terms. This flies in the face of our 21st century tax hustle, where some pour in vast amounts, some chip in a little, and the rest… nothing.

In *Appendix C*, you will find language in the U.S. Constitution requiring direct taxes to be apportioned equally.

The New London and New Haven Colonies

As these events transpired along the pristine Connecticut river, two further independent Connecticut colonies formed: New Haven and New London. The New Haven Colony's purpose dealt with certain religious practices these settlers wanted, not part of Winthrop Sr.'s practices up north in Massachusetts. New London's core centered around the commercial ambitions of John Winthrop Jr.

Winthrop Jr. (above)—son of Boston's founder Winthrop Sr., wanted to grow his own garden, not his father's, so he sailed around the bend and claimed an area at the mouth of a small river. He named the river the Thames, after England's Thames, and named his colony New London, just as London, England sits upon the Thames. Clearly, Winthrop Jr. set his sights on Mother England.

Because the Winthrop's were lawyers, they cared about making things legal, including property rights and title to property. Winthrop Jr. wanted to secure his claimed property in the New London area and knew no controlling legal authority existed with which to achieve this. So, he invented a controlling legal authority by going straight to the top—Charles II, King of England.

In 1661, Winthrop Jr. and some 10 of his cohorts sailed to London and obtained an audience with the King. The King recently came to power due to his *Royalist* forces defeating the anti-Royalist *Roundheads* in the protracted English Civil War. During these years of strife in England, no one cared about activities occurring in the God-forsaken wilderness of America, and so, the King had no framework.

Winthrop Jr. explained the colonial situation to the King, and spelled out the King's own interest in the matter. The King was all ears for Winthrop to propose a model for handling the colonies and Winthrop Jr. just happened to have such a model in his back pocket. All the King needed to do was sign it, and he did. The document's name? *The Charles II Connecticut Charter.*

What did the charter say? Let us quote the writing of Bruce P. Stark, as excerpted from "Connecticut History and Culture":

The Charter was an extraordinary document because it gave the people of Connecticut a clear legal basis for their colony, provided for the absorption of New Haven Colony, and, most importantly, granted the "Governour and Company of the English Colony of Connecticut in New England in America" an exceedingly generous degree of self-government.

By the Charter, Charles II created a corporation. The members of this corporation were the freemen of Connecticut, and the company was granted complete freedom to lease, grant, sell, bargain, alienate, and dispose of property as other corporations had the right to do.

The Charter provided for a governor, deputy-governor and 12 assistants, all of whom were to be elected annually by the freemen of the company. An Assembly consisting of not more than two representatives from each town elected by the freemen was to meet twice annually to act upon the business of the corporation. All legislative and judicial power was granted to the General Assembly with the reservation that the General Assembly could enact no laws contrary to those of England.

The land tenure granted to the freemen of Connecticut was that of the "Manor of East Greenwich in Free and Comon Sociage," the freest in England, in return for which the king was to receive one-fifth of all gold and silver mined in the colony.

The Charter established Narragansett Bay as the eastern boundary of the colony and the "South Sea," the Pacific Ocean, as the western boundary.

One key clause—*That the General Assembly could enact no laws contrary to those of England,* means that the greatest law of England—that the King held allodial title to all the land within his kingdom—can be used at any time to trump the rights just granted by the charter.

Remember, under the Divine Right of Kings system, "allodial" means granted by God to the Monarch. All other rights to land by others are feudal, beholden to the king.

By feudal, the monarch's land grants remained *limited and conditional*, requiring the tenant to stay in good standing with the overlord. For example, in the 1770's these allodial rights suddenly slapped America in the face when the King quartered soldiers in homes, seeking to collect taxes—a strictly legal proceeding!

When Winthrop returned with the Charter in hand, he met instinctive pushback from many. But Winthrop possessed hard backup. For the first time ever, the English Crown sent warships to New England—the mission: let everyone know the Charter meant business, and, one more thing: after stopping in Massachusetts, Rhode Island, and Connecticut, the fleet, in 1664, continued to New Amsterdam (New York), demanding the Dutch governor surrender, which he did. New York remained in the English fold thereafter.

King Phillip's War 1675-1678

Yes, the fleet stopped by, but for the most part, Americans survived, left alone in the wilderness without any English resources in sight.

By 1675, the colonial population across New England had grown to 80,000, with Native American populations dwindling to 10,000, mainly due to disease and inter-tribal warfare. In total, 110 English/Puritan towns stood, half in Massachusetts, the others in Rhode Island and Connecticut.

Metacomet—who called himself "King Phillip"—presided as chief of the Wampanoag Confederacy, a longstanding ally of the Plymouth Colony, ever since the beginning with William Bradford as governor and Standish as military captain. But by 1675 relations soured, and Plymouth stopped engaging the Indians, with settlers taking Indian land without compensation.

Other slights also took place and Metacomet mobilized the confederacy. In the end, half of the English towns burnt to the ground (including my town of Simsbury), with 1,000 English and 3,000 Indian dead. Uncas, it is noted, fought with the English, as did other tribes.

This resulted in an unintended consequence: the colonists' successful defense of New England using their own resources brought them to the attention of the British royal government, which did nothing to support the colonists, but instead realized that the colonies could become problematic.

The Charter Oak Incident 1687

The Crown reviewed the various Charles II charters (not just Connecticut's) and found them too lenient. This led to the Charter Oak incident in Hartford, Connecticut.

Connecticuthistory.org describes the incident as follows:

Charles's II death in 1685 brought his brother, James II, to the throne. James disapproved of the Royal Charters and demanded their return. The charters interfered with James's plan to establish the Dominion of New England—a combination of the New England colonies and the colony of New York under the leadership of one royal official.

In 1687, Sir Edmond Andros, the Royal Governor of the Dominion, met with leaders of the Connecticut colony in Hartford. Debates continued for hours as the colonists steadfastly refused to give up the Charter. According to legend, all of the candles in the meeting house suddenly blew out and, during the confusion, the Charter disappeared. It was hidden in the trunk of a large white oak tree where it was protected from the King and from Andros.

Despite Connecticut's resistance, it became part of the Dominion of New England for the next two years. In 1689 James II was overthrown and Andros lost power in the colonies. The Connecticut Charter emerged from hiding and was used to govern Connecticut until 1818.

Please recall that the Charles II Charter is referred to 100 years later in the 1793 property rights statute of Connecticut.

French and Indian Wars 1702-1765

In the 1700s, England and France fought on an almost continual basis, starting with Queen Ann's War in 1702, with most of the blood spilling in Europe, as well as much in America. The French in America developed a hunting/trapping economy, whereas the English chose farming. This made the English towns sitting ducks for both the forest-roaming French and their Indian allies.

In New England, the French sent Iroquois from the west, enemies of the New England tribes, into English towns to do their worst. In February of 1704, Jean-Baptiste Hertel de Rouville and an Indian entourage attacked the English frontier settlement at Deerfield, Massachusetts, just before dawn, burning part of the town, killing 47, and carting off 30 women and children, never to be seen again.

Using various Indian allies, the French attacks, similar to those in New England, ran down the Eastern seaboard, and as with the various Indian wars of the 1600's, settlers formed their own militias to defend themselves, without help from the Crown. The most famous homegrown force emerged from Virginia under George Washington, who penetrated deep into French territory, killing many, and making Washington the natural leader in what remained to come.

The "Call to Arms" flier drawn and printed by Benjamin Franklin.

By 1754, the level of warfare with France grew to larger proportions, and British forces arrived from Europe to lead the homegrown troops.

Connecticut sent 23,000 volunteers, 12 percent of the colony's population, to fight in the Hudson valley. Below, from ConnecticutHistory.Org, David Drury, a retired editor of the *Hartford Courant*—describes the price of the French wars.

The end of the war found the colony economically depressed and deeply in debt—and it only got worse. The British government had to find a way to pay costs associated with the war (which nearly doubled Britain's national debt). The ministers determined that the American colonies needed to share in the expense since they greatly benefited from the war's outcome. First came tariffs on sugar, coffee, wine, and other imported commodities. Then, in 1765, Parliament adopted the notorious Stamp Act, effectively taxing all paper materials. The colonies exploded into opposition.

Next...the American Revolution—The biggest explosion ever!

Below: Colonel Samuel Selden, Lyme, Connecticut, to Captain Joshua Huntington, calling for reinforcements to be sent to New York City, July 6th, 1776:

Rouse the People to see their Danger. Stir them up by all that is dear in this life. Our Wives, our Children, our property, our Liberty is at Stake....

The anti-British fever in Connecticut ran hot. Before the first shots were fired, the colony passed anti-Tory laws, threatening citizens loyal to England with imprisonment. Many fled.

The longstanding separatist population, backed by the Charles II charter, wanted no part of the crown's overlord behavior, and despite its status as one of the smallest colonies to participate in the Revolution, Connecticut fielded 40,000 men—a fifth of its population—and a great deal of armaments—thus deemed the *Provision State.* Indeed, Connecticut, entering the war "whole hog," produced a larger proportion of food consumed by the continental Army than any other state.

From the Society of the Cincinnati, founded in 1783 by officers of the Continental Army:

In addition to providing manpower and ships, Connecticut was the leading supplier of food, clothing, and munitions for the Continental Army, earning the nickname "The Provisions State." In April 1775, the General Assembly established a commissariat to "supply all necessary Stores and provisions for the troops now to be raised for the Defense of this Colony."

Nine regional commissaries were set up inside Connecticut to procure, store, and distribute such items as food, cloth, tents and other camp equipment, lead, bullets, and gunpowder.

Joseph Trumbull (1738-1778), the Connecticut governor's oldest son, was appointed head of the Commissary Department and was sent with the militia to Boston to oversee supply operations. So impressed was General Washington with Trumbull's performance that he recommended to Congress his appointment as Commissary General of the Continental Army in July 1775.

Concurrent to provisions, solidarity amongst Connecticut's citizenry against the Crown uniquely extended to the top. Again, from the Society of the Cincinnati:

Succeeding to the governorship in 1769, Trumbull would become the only colonial governor to champion the patriots' cause, remaining in office through the years of the Revolution. Under his leadership, Connecticut became a key force in the struggle for national independence.

As stated, Connecticut went to the war "whole hog," and, at the war's end, its citizens sought their prize in the form of liberty stemming from absolute rights over one's property.

With this said, ill treatment of those Americans loyal to the King meant that not all property was respected. Britain's requirement in signing The Treaty of Paris—recognizing America's independence—included a provision protecting the lands held by American loyalists.

At war's end, in Connecticut, absolute property rights, unencumbered ownership, true independence, and liberty prevailed. Slavery, though, continued for a time. Connecticut's Gradual Abolition Act of 1784 did not emancipate any enslaved persons, only those who would be born into slavery and only after they reached the age of 25.

Historical Summary

A Connecticut-specific mindset reflecting 150 years of colonial struggle certainly prevailed in the common farmer at the end of the Revolution, and this heritage remains today part of the *Law of the Land.*

But sitting above grassroots aspirations for owning farm land, the founders also forged a national-level philosophy on property, their ideas today also part of the *Law of the Land.* We explain next how the federal government organized to protect the people's freedom (their precious property and natural rights) while not interfering with the allowed law-making powers of the states in *Chapter 6— Founding Principles.*

In the PRESS,
and speedily will be published,
THE

FEDERALIST,

A Collection of Essays written in favor of the New Constitution.

By a Citizen of New-York.

Corrected by the Author, with Additions and Alterations.

This work will be printed on a fine Paper and good Type, in one handsome Volume duodecimo, and delivered to subscribers at the moderate price of one dollar. A few copies will be printed on superfine royal writing paper, price ten shillings.
No money required till delivery.

To render this work more complete, will be added, without any additional expence,

PHILO-PUBLIUS,

AND THE

Articles of the Convention,

As agreed upon at Philadelphia, September 17th, 1787.

Chapter 6

America's Founding Principles

Now we will delve into the crux of property rights, as understood by America's founders.

Europe was created by history. America was created by philosophy.—**Margret Thatcher**

Chapter 5—Connecticut's Historical Context, which you just read, all blood and guts, tomahawks, and strife—covered the time leading up to the American Revolution: colonists running an excruciating gauntlet. The Connecticut Yankees who ran the gauntlet concluded: *It is my land!* And they said so, loudly, in print, by passing the 1793 Property Rights Act, now CGS 47-1.

In parallel to Connecticut's historical struggles leading to its property rights statute, an umbrella cerebral approach justifying *It is my land* took place amongst the founders at a national level. And as Margret Thatcher said, the American constitutional framers had philosophic minds, and rather than by accident, America assembled itself upon thoughtful concepts. This chapter, *Chapter 6—Founding Principles,* examines property rights and *Law of the Land* from this cerebral perch.

First off, some people, mainly on the Modern Left, claim that none of the principles described next matter, though cast in stone within Common Law, the U.S. Constitution, and Connecticut state law books. These anti-law advocates insist that human conditions in the modern era have so lapped the primitive ideas of 1793 that older legal directives no longer apply; moreover, they are laughable, especially where concerning private property rights and property taxation.

Even a reflective Thomas Jefferson, then in his seventh decade, commented…

Some men look at constitutions with sanctimonious reverence and deem them like the Ark of the Covenant, too sacred to be touched.

They ascribe to the men of the preceding age wisdom more than human, and suppose what they did to be beyond amendment. I know that age well; I belonged to it and labored with it. It deserved well of its country. It was very like the present; and forty years of experience in government is worth a century of book reading; and this they would themselves would say, were they to rise from the dead… Laws and institutions must go hand in hand with the progress of the human mind…

So Jefferson favors flexibility as times change… but *any* change?

As will be seen, within Common Law, the U.S. Constitution, and Connecticut state statutes, one's rights to property are absolute, unencumbered by taxes or rules—natural rights sitting above the law. Whereas in the modern socialist view, title to property only provides the title holder with limited rights set by the whims and mercy of the government. Yes, you "own" it, but you can only use it our way, and you owe taxes doing it our way. More so, if you do not comply, the government can arrest you and/or confiscate the property. More on socialism later…

Actually, today's 21st century limited rights situation sounds very much similar to the old 1500's Monarchy situation. I doubt Jefferson would have considered property right encroachment some sort of necessary "progress"—throwing the baby (absolute property rights and Due Process) out with the bathwater (the need to fund government schools).

In the 21st century, both town and state employees (our modern Sheriffs of Nottingham) enforce this heavy-duty paradigm of gouging civilization's wealth via property taxes, arrogantly asserting themselves without any laws sanctifying their authority.

Tax collectors and local judges simply believe they have standing, assuming the law. How this willful illusion became weaved into our governing fiber will be discussed later.

But for now, *Chapter 6—America's Founding Principles*, simply sets forth the philosophies behind the property laws that actually exist on the books today, yet remain ignored.

What *are* property rights, let's review?

As already mentioned, property rights describe what you can do with your property. If a car, you have the right to paint it a new color. If a pond, you can fish in it. If a house, you can add a room to it...

Property rights are absolute when no restriction exists on what you can do with your property. If one needs a permit to add a room to a home, then one does not enjoy absolute rights. If you can fish, but need to pay taxes on the pond to do so, that is not absolute ownership.

One, obviously, can have title, though one's use of the property is limited. In the days of the English King, one might have perpetual or time-bound title to some farm land, but the King still kept allodial title, meaning he could confiscate, tax, or regulate your use of the otherwise-titled land. But you, not someone else, held that particular title, with whatever caveats suited the overlord.

Property title philosophy—*absolute* property rights versus mere *limited* rights—sits at the center of the formation of the United States.

Time to dig in. And as Thatcher reminds us, it all starts with philosophy. Enter John Locke...

John Locke's *Two Treatises of Government*

Among the natural rights of the colonists are these: First a right to life, secondly to liberty, and thirdly to property; together with the right to defend them in the best manner they can. **Sam Adams**

Where did Sam Adams, a key American founder, get this idea?

"It is one thing to show a man
that he is in error, and another to
put him in possession of truth."
~ John Locke

Other than the protest of the tea tax, most Americans today know little about the original thinking and philosophical views of the founders—ideas that fueled the American Revolution and make America unique—an exception of human history.

Everyone considers Washington the Father of America (and that's because he was), the place where, if you wanted to, you could make something of yourself. It was up to you, and no one was necessarily expected to help you. Some perhaps would, but no one had to. It was up to you. This wasn't for everybody, but in the early years those who were game—such as the Connecticut separatists—did whatever it took to come here and try.

But few people know who *John Locke* was, even though Locke, an Englishman, served as the dominant intellectual influence for all of the founding fathers, including Washington.

Key founders, you recall, include:

- *George Washington* — the Father, he won the war, and presided over the young country;

- *Benjamin Franklin* — the Role Model, he created and embodied the idea and character of what it is to be an American;

- *Thomas Jefferson* — the Artist, he painted the dream of America in words;

- *John Adams* — the Dealmaker, behind the scenes everywhere, including in Paris when the English signed papers giving up claim to the colonies;

- *Alexander Hamilton* — the Operations Visionary, knowing what worked in the day-to-day running of a country;

- *John Jay*—the Lawyer, and first Chief Justice;

- **Sam Adams**—the Activist, infusing rebellion amongst the people;

- **Patrick Henry**—the Orator, giving voice to the movement, "Give me liberty or give me death";

- **Thomas Paine**—the "Pamphleteer," keeping the people engaged;

- **John Hancock**—the Financier, organizing and funding resistance against Britain;

- **Roger Sherman**—the Observer, sitting on every committee to spot the missed point, the unintended consequence; and

- **James Madison**—the Architect, the one who formulated the very structure of the United States by drafting the U.S. Constitution.

They were all Locke guys.

John Locke lived from 1632-1704, long before the founders, and published his now not-so-famous, yet earth-shattering work, *Two Treatises of Government*. In it, he explains to the world how humanity has evolved until then, what it all meant so far, and what humans should do next if they are to fulfill their God-given potential.

Locke charts out the relationship of property and ownership to human freedom. In a nutshell, I present his late 1600's vision:

Human Faculties Endowed by the Creator

Similar to *Descartes*, Locke begins with the premise that humans exist as extensions of God, endowed with divine spirit. Our only true superior, therefore, is God (as our spirit is an extension of His), and so, any impingement of one person by another is inherently against the deepest desire of God's divine will. God did not create us, each personally, just to have us enslave, lord over, or bully each other.

As Washington said: "We don't need masters."

When God gave man His spirit, he included certain spiritually fueled faculties. These human faculties sit way above the purely mental abilities possessed by other animal species on the planet.

Whereas other animals only live in the moment within nature, and even then in specific biospheres that sustain them, humans use their special faculties to operate within time and to transform natural resources into things useful toward supporting their lives—no matter upon which corner of the earth we decide to dwell.

Only humans possess faculties for language, history, mathematics, physics, chemistry, biology, art, music, literature, philosophy, religion, architecture, engineering, agriculture, the transformation of basic foods into cuisine, knowledge accumulation and breakthroughs, fabrication of tools and the physical dexterity to use them, and other faculties, including warfare and the ability to breed other species.

These faculties, which exist nowhere else in nature, therefore did not result from a micro-Darwinian mutation of some pre-human ape. According to the American founders, the faculty to understand things, comes, inductively, from the fact that humans are endowed with spirit, allowing us to tap into the divine mind of God.

Once one fathoms the existence of a spiritual *connection*, one quickly sees that our unique faculties come from the spiritual *dimension*, and not from our ancestral gene pool. Sure, we get other stuff from the gene pool, like hair, but not *this* stuff.

Labor

Humans possess an even higher trait called labor, something that allows humans to blend and apply all of these special faculties together toward one's survival, and more so, toward one's moral and temporal well-being.

For example, 10 acres of virgin forest represents only so much raw survival potential—a couple of squirrels, maybe. But through labor, we can transform this land into an agricultural resource that can feed and sustain many. Human labor, Locke argues, has so leveraged the bounty of nature that 99½ percent of what humans hold as valuable comes from the infusion of human labor into nature, and only one-half of one percent comes from raw nature itself.

And so, regardless of the proportions, we humans labor to improve our lot in life. But different people, cultures, and nations all choose different degrees of labor they are willing to infuse, because with labor comes "the pain of labor."

Property, according to Locke, stems from the above, consisting of the three things you inherently own: your life (no one can own you, you come from God), your material goods and land (no one should take the fruits of your labor, the result of the pain you were willing to infuse), and your liberties (no one should limit your choices for disposing of your life, land, or goods).

Property, in the broadest sense, when owned absolutely, is freedom itself. Most of Locke's writing then qualifies this by explaining how all of the freedom/property stuff sits inside a body of laws, but even here he speaks of a narrow set of laws prohibiting one from compromising another's property.

Property Rights & Thomas Jefferson

Ok, so we have property. But does one, even after exerting painful labor into the creation of property, hold absolute rights to this property? According to the English Kings, the answer is "no." And so we need a special person, say a Thomas Jefferson, to unravel the rope.

Jefferson's dissertation follows. He focuses on what we call "Common Law," the unwritten law that English people lived by for centuries. Even today in America, should no constitutional or statutory directive exist on a topic, we cite old Common Law.

Jefferson points out that in old England, before William the Conqueror took over in 1066 and introduced "French" feudal title claims to property, that the property rights held under Anglo Saxon Common Law stood absolute and allodial (no feudal duties owed to any other person).

Moreover, when the Conqueror installed feudal claims to English land, he did not claim all lands, as many estates still remained with Anglo Saxon lords under the Common Law system of allodial rights. Jefferson's words:

That we shall at this time also take notice of an error in the nature of our landholdings, which crept in at a very early period of our settlement. The introduction of the feudal tenures (land controlled by a monarch) *into the kingdom of England, though ancient, is well enough understood to set this matter in its proper light.*

In the earlier ages of the Saxon settlement feudal holdings were certainly altogether unknown, and very few, if any, had been introduced at the time of the Norman conquest.

Our Saxon ancestors (prior to 1066) *held their lands, as they did their personal property, in absolute dominion, disencumbered with any superior.*

William the Conqueror first introduced that system [feudalism] generally.

The lands which had belonged to those who fell at the battle of Hastings, and in the subsequent insurrections of his reign, formed a considerable proportion of the lands of the whole kingdom. These he granted out, subject to feudal duties, as did he also those of a great number of his new subjects, who by persuasions or threats were induced to surrender then for that purpose. But still much of the land was left in the hands of his Saxon subjects, held of no superior, and not subject to feudal conditions.

A general principle indeed was introduced that "all lands in England were held either mediately or immediately of the crown": but thus was borrowed from those holdings which were truly feudal, and applied to others for the purposes of illustration.

Feudal holdings were therefore but exceptions out of the Saxon laws of possession, under which all lands were held in absolute right. These therefore still form the basis of the common law, to prevail whenever the exceptions have not taken place.

America was not conquered by William the Norman, nor its lands surrendered to him or any of his successors. Possessions are undoubtedly of the [absolute disencumbered] nature.

Our ancestors however, were laborers, not lawyers. The fictitious principle that all lands belong originally to the king, that they were early persuaded to believe real, and accordingly took grants of their own lands from the crown. And while the crown continued to grant for small sums and on reasonable rents, there was no inducement to arrest the error.

Boy oh boy, Jefferson could really figure stuff out! The King made it all up; he never had a feudal claim on American soil, as we never surrendered our land to him. John Winthrop Jr. tricked everyone for his own land grab agenda.

But through the Hasting's surrender, a *myth* slowly took hold, a con, called the Divine Right of Kings, claiming that all rights, liberties, and properties across the land belonged to the king. The king alone had allodial title; he merely permitted subjects to use his possessions.

Locke and Jefferson debunked this audacity.

And Thomas Paine's *Common Sense* publication explained it. Read these first sentences to his famous 40-page pamphlet explaining how the king Hoodwinked his subjects without being noticed:

Perhaps the sentiments contained in the following pages are not yet sufficiently fashionable to procure them general favor; a long habit of not thinking a thing wrong, gives it a superficial appearance of being right. But the tumult soon subsides. Time makes more converts than reason. **Paine**

English Common Law

Of note: Jefferson's statement that *"Our Saxon ancestors held their lands, as they did their personal property, in absolute dominion, disencumbered with any superior,"* is echoed in CGS 47-1. Its sentiment is part of the American *Law of the Land*.

In referring to his Saxon ancestors, Jefferson means a great deal, as a Saxon held vast natural rights.

Winston Churchill, in his *History of the English-Speaking Peoples* describes the "freeman" rights of the Engle, Saxon, and Jute tribes who moved into England when Rome departed around 400 A.D. as follows.

Within this society of "freemen," each person together with their fixed and movable property, controls himself, with no obligation to the chief. One's allegiance to the chief stays voluntary, primarily concerned with defense of the community and nothing else. The Saxon Freemen's right to allodial autonomy—encompassing one's property—becomes the foundation of English Common Law, law still in effect in both the United Kingdom and the United States today.
Churchill

The English Freemen carried on in this allodial manner up until 1066, when the French Normans took over and instilled feudal arrangements across the land. For the next several centuries, the old English allodial guard pushed back against feudalism, starting in 1215 with the Magna Carta, then the English Civil War in the 1600's, reaching equilibrium during the Glorious Revolution of 1688, when Parliament gained many powers.

The United States, by its adoption of old English Common law, shares in this legacy of natural, absolute rights to property.

To be thorough, one needs to peer into the English Magna Carta of 1215, even for a moment. Besides giving the lesser nobles rights under the King, it reaches back into English Common Law for the little guys, too. Consider:

No freeman shall be taken or imprisoned or diseased, or exiled or in any way destroyed, nor will we go upon him or send upon him, except by the lawful judgment of his peers or the Law of the Land ... from the **Magna Carta**.

This *Law of the Land* does not refer to written laws. It refers to one's natural rights sitting separate and above the reach of government. As you will soon read, Common Law rights, some of them set forth in the Magna Carta, are preserved in our Bill of Rights.

The Declaration of Independence

This document, written by Jefferson, tweaked by Adams and Franklin, and signed by the 13 colony representatives about to endure seven years of warfare with England... merges Locke's philosophies and Jefferson's ability to blend philosophy with historical context.

The first part of the Declaration is pure Locke:

We hold these truths to be self-evident, that all men are created equal, that they are endowed by their Creator with certain unalienable Rights, that among these are Life, Liberty and the pursuit of Happiness.—That to secure these rights, Governments are instituted among Men, deriving their just powers from the consent of the governed...

Next comes the long and exhaustive list of grievances, spelled out by Jefferson, so that mankind can understand the course of action the colonies will undertake:

...a decent respect to the opinions of mankind requires that they should declare the causes which impel them to the separation.

Once the unfathomable list of grievances concludes, Jefferson closes with:

We, therefore, the Representatives of the United States of America, in General Congress, Assembled, appealing to the Supreme Judge of the world for the rectitude of our intentions, do, in the Name, and by Authority of the good People of these Colonies, solemnly publish and declare,

That these united Colonies are, and of Right ought to be Free and Independent States, that they are Absolved from all Allegiance to the British Crown, and that all political connection between them and the State of Great Britain, is and ought to be totally dissolved; and that as Free and Independent States, they have full Power to levy War, conclude Peace, contract Alliances, establish Commerce, and to do all other Acts and Things which Independent States may of right do.—And for the support of this Declaration, with a firm reliance on the protection of Divine Providence, we mutually pledge to each other our Lives, our Fortunes, and our sacred Honor.

Next, state by state, come the famous signatures.

None of these high-quality patriots accepted the coming terrors of war with the idea that the new American government created in England's place should someday reinstate the very oppression they sought to escape. Government control of ourselves and our extended selves—our property—would be shut down for good. Life, Liberty, and Property would stand as the new *Law of the Land*... or so they thought.

Deists

One fallacy about the founders ties them to Christianity, or at least religious freedom. Actually, their goal centered on protecting people and their property from religions and religion-infused governments, and to protect one in holding one's beliefs (part of their Property).

Here's the shocker: the founders did not often go to church, they cringed at Christianity and the Trinity; they believed in divine spirit (obviously, based upon their documents), but with the deity having no direct relationship with people. The founders were what are called *Deists*, accepting the power of spiritually-fueled intellect, yet crafting policy focused on our lives and our property while living in nature on Earth.

The following quotes illustrate that the founding Deists championed individuality, liberty, and property ownership, and did not focus on making things safe for Christianity.

The God who gave us life, gave us liberty
at the same time. **Jefferson**

God is an essence we know nothing of. **Adams**

He has given us reason to find out the truth, and the real
design and true end of our existence. **Adams**

God helps those who help themselves. **Franklin**

And, more directly: *Is it because you are sunk in the cruelty of superstition, or feel no interest in the honor of your Creator, that you listen to the horrid tales of the Bible, or hear them with callous indifference?"* **Paine**

Asked about his conception of God, **Lincoln** replied:

The same as my conception of nature. That it is impossible
for either to be personal.

These Deists, these Founders (and Lincoln), did not merely wing it. In so many ways, our small unit of revolutionaries read from the same page, especially in the areas of religion and philosophy.

Quite a team, equal to the Greek warrior/policy visionaries at Troy (Odysseus, Achilles, et., al.). And besides Locke and the Greeks, the founders grappled with the philosophical luminaries of their time, like Rousseau (a socialist) and Montesquieu (who advocated for the separation of powers between Legislative, Executive and Judicial branches).

Somehow, our team of founders won the war with England, held the center, collaborated amongst themselves—for an extended number of years—and sorted things out, finally promoting a new constitution to the people they had sworn to represent.

The U.S. Constitution

The Constitution was not written overnight. Out of the amazing list of founding fathers mentioned above, three nuts-and-bolts guys took the lead, largely Madison, as supported by Hamilton and Jay. Published dialogue amongst the three became known as the Federalist Papers, with Hamilton the most outspoken.

The Federalist Papers crafted the essential features for assembling a federal government that kept the states as independent as possible. With this the goal, the debate centered on where to draw the line between federal and state authority.

Before the U.S. Constitution, the states, during the Revolution years, operated under The Articles of Confederation. This arrangement left the central government weak. States could "opt out" of things like paying money toward the war.

During the war, Hamilton, a battlefield commander and member of Washington's personal staff, experienced the small-minded stinginess of the states that allowed the military to starve at Valley Forge. And so, he argued heavily for central governmental power over the states.

Yet no one questioned that once the central (federal) government was provisioned properly, all other matters should remain with the states... *except for the following.*

The highest ideal for American government remained that the government should serve the people and not the opposite.

To solve this, the interplay between the states and the federal government needed one more safety measure: *The Bill of Rights*, designed to protect the individual from overreach and abuse of power by either state or federal authorities. The key protections are the Due Process clauses which reach back to the Magna Carta, claiming the natural rights one enjoys separate and above written law.

In addition to certain famous rights such as Freedom of Speech (again, opinion part of your property) and Freedom of Religion (belief also part of your property), much of the Bill of Rights deals with protecting any form of property from said abuse. The people demanded these protections in writing as amendments to the originally proposed Constitution draft. Ten amendments surfaced; six, besides Speech and Religion, also relate to property as follows:

The 3rd Amendment—No soldier shall in times of peace be quartered in any house, without consent of the owner, nor in times of war, but in a manner prescribed by law.

The 4th Amendment—The rights of people to be secure in their persons, houses, and effects against unreasonable searches and seizures shall not be violated and no warrants shall issue, but upon probable cause...

The 5th Amendment—Nor shall [anyone] be deprived of life, liberty, or property without due process of law; Nor shall private property be taken for public use without just compensation.

The 7th, 9th, and 10th Amendments preserve "absolute" Common Law property rights for the individual for any subjects not specifically delegated to the government.

The 7th Amendment—No fact tried by a jury, shall be otherwise re- examined in any court of the United States than according to common law. The 9th Amendment—The enumeration (listing) of certain rights, shall not be construed to deny or disparage others retained by the people.

The 10th Amendment—The powers not delegated to the United States by the Constitution, nor prohibited by it to the states are reserved to the states and the people.

And so... due to Common Law property rights, backed by due process guarantees, backed by absolute rights cemented in CGS 47-1... in the first decades of the United States, clearly until the Civil War, individuals owned property in absolute terms, and they meant it! "Hey, hey, you, you, get off of my cloud" was the *Law of the Land.*

So what happened? *Chapter 7—Legalized Plunder,* comes next. But first a word about "Liberalism," a word co-opted today by the Left. I present my definition:

***Liberalism** first became a political movement during the age of enlightenment, in the 1600's and 1700's. Liberalism rejected the notions of hereditary privilege, state religion, absolute monarchy, and the Divine Right of Kings. Each man has a natural right to life, liberty and property. According to the social contract, governments must not violate these rights.*

Liberalism replaced absolutism with representative democracy and the rule of law. Since that time, Liberalism grew to include the government's role of engineering solutions to social and economic problems that cannot be solved in any other manner, so long as those solutions do not compromise the rights, wealth, and property of individuals.

Franklin (with Adams) looking over Jefferson's draft of the Declaration of Independence.

Thomas Paine—Pamphleteer

Chapter 7

Legalized Plunder

Finally, we look the problem in the eye, and some might push back...

The policy of American government is to leave its citizens free, neither restraining them nor aiding them in their pursuits. **Thomas Jefferson**

Some 200 years later...

We are fast approaching the stage of the ultimate inversion: the stage where the government is free to do anything it pleases, while the citizens may act only by permission; which is the stage of the darkest periods of human history, the stage of rule by brute force. **Ayn Rand**

Socialism

The American Left grew slowly, and certainly not with Jefferson, founder of the Democrat Party. The determined attack on private property took place after the American Civil War, once immigration accelerated, continuing through today. Overall, property right erosion became a major weapon within the Socialist arsenal.

Having just defined Liberalism, I should next propose my definition of Socialism.

Socialism first became a distinct political movement during the Social Revolution Era, the mid-1800's. Socialism calls for public rather than private control of property and natural resources—through the authority of government to own, aggressively tax, and regulate—with individuals not existing individually, but living in a cooperative system.

Socialism considers everything people produce a social product, with everyone in that society entitled to share in it. Society as a whole, through a pyramid of command, controls individuals and property for the benefit of all its members. Government can compromise the individual to achieve these goals.

Similar to a cancer, American Socialism spread quietly, infiltrating centers of power within the American civilization—entertainment, media, education, the money supply, the courts, property rights, etc.—finally corrupting the minds of the people, making many afraid to tap into the possibilities of independence through personal pursuit. And, to mask things, today's stealth Socialists cleverly label themselves Liberals.

But at the founding, the American system solely cherished independence and freedom, and this meant assignment of "absolute rights" to property. The snail-like schism taking place over the next 225 years saw laws protecting property stay fairly consistent; it was government administration that veered left, leaving the rule of law behind.

Some of the stealth tools used by our Socialist government include federal and state income taxation, unchecked debt issuance, anything-goes land taxation, unfunded mandates, regulations, executive orders, and, oh, "code"—the wall of rules (regulations) written by bureaucrats, not voted upon by the people or their representatives in state and federal legislatures.

The whole of it operates as a spider web capturing our freedoms, even though law guarantees our freedoms—our properties. And because property rights provide the very ballast for the John Locke-American freedom model, they required suppression with a special strategy. And a good one presented itself: "Caring for the children", especially the millions coming in from foreign countries, flocking to the cities during the late 1800's and early 1900's, and flocking once again from Central America.

Government Schools

The education of all children, from the moment they can get along without a mother's care, shall be in state institutions.
—**Karl Marx**

As mentioned in *Chapter 4—CGS 47-1*, the evolving driver behind property taxation is the government school conundrum.

Similar to the *Military-Industrial Complex*, of which President Eisenhower warned us as he retired from office, another hard-to-stop conspiracy is the *Government School-Indoctrination Complex* that seduces families with zero-cost education for their children, puts power into the hands of teacher union bosses, and slips Socialist-leaning teachers into the classroom and the boards of education, all the while bowing to state and federal dictates.

An American School House prior to World War II

And the government pays for it by taxing our houses! In my town, there once stood a dozen school houses, paid for by the families. By World War II, these were somehow retired and replaced with the property-tax-fueled government schools. How did they pull this off?

Slowly. Though the local government issued tax bills before the Civil War, the farmers refused to pay them. Yet after the war, a two-step process began to close the deal, moving quietly and keeping them ignorant.

Previously I mentioned that forces altered CGS 47-1 over time. From 1793 onward, the statute stayed whole... until 1866. In 1866, Connecticut published a new statute book, and its preamble advised the members of the legislature—who would ratify the edition *en masse*—that clerical analysts (code writers, directed by someone, possibly not even a legislator) removed "unnecessary language" from certain unspecified statutes.

Sure enough, CGS 47-1 was one of these "certain unspecified statutes." The code writers dropped the word "allodial" and the entire first paragraph explaining the change in property rights due to our freedom from the King. You may recall that "allodial" meant that we acquired our absolute property rights as citizens from God, not from man or government.

By dropping allodial, CGS 47-1 still promised absolute rights, but also set up the possibility that government favor, not God's divine will, makes this possible—the greatest shell game ever executed.

Second, 10 years later, in 1875, the Connecticut state legislature passed the property tax statutes. Now that God has been removed, the state began to chip away at absolute rights, turning them into limited rights. Who can complain? After all, it is for the children, and it is not much.

One could still hold title to one's fishing pond and fish there— and post no fishing signs all around the property —- but only if you paid an annual tribute to the new overlord: the municipality. If you don't pay, the municipality can slap a tax lien on the property, sell it on the cheap to extract its extortion money, and there goes your fishing pond.

But the amount of tax assessed and paid back then comprised mere pennies.

Facing the threat of losing everything they had, none of the little farmers working across Connecticut in 1875 possessed the wealth or education to counter this audacity. Plus, it was only pennies, and no one fathomed the distinction between private property and commercial business (which can be taxed). Everyone fell in line and paid up, and no one has yet broken ranks, even to this day.

Until now, that is. As you will soon read, a few brave Connecticut souls have recently gone to court over this. It is no longer pennies. But before examining these recent pushback actions, let's pause and review the tax lien statute. Just because it became law does not make it legal on three mechanical accounts.

- There are no broken contracts between the property owner and the municipality. The whole concept of a lien is to freeze assets until a contract dispute is cleared up. With taxation, no contract existed in the first place, so no dispute; liens do not belong here.

- Procedurally, to get a lien, one must go to court and present one's situation to a judge—the due process clause in the Bill of Rights—so that the judge can determine IF a true contract breach appears in play before authorizing a court-signed lien. Yet rather than judges, municipalities simply mail a lien notice to the property owner threatening confiscation.

- Any new statute in conflict with established law, without first retiring prior law, makes the newer statute conflicted, difficult to enforce. The 1875 lien statute—should it be applied to private homes—stands in conflict with prior property rights statute passed in 1793. Statute 47-1 happens to protect the owner from outside encumbrance—of which the lien extortion is a prime example.

And moving up to the level of U.S. Constitution, as explained previously, we find the tax lien flagrantly defying due process protection of one's Life, Liberty, and Property against government encumbrance.

Property versus Commercial Taxation

Before moving on, we ought review the rules of taxation in America.

Recall that the Constitution spells out the government's power, including the power to levy tax. In the early years, the government levied taxes on commercial activities, such as imports arriving from other countries. Only in 1913 did the government add one's income—from any source—to the list of commercial activities via the 16th Amendment.

Owning property *is not a commercial activity*; selling property is. While owning your home, things like products, services, rents, loans, and labor are *not* being exchanged for money; there is no *indirect* commercial activity to tax. The topic of *indirect* (one has some choice) and *direct* (no choice) taxation is covered in *Appendix C*.

One interesting case in the 1800's dealt with a man who put up a billboard on his property to sell advertising. When he received a tax bill, the owner claimed he did not owe tax on the billboard because the billboard stood on private property. The owner lost the case because he engaged in commercial activity on his property, not because his property itself was taxable. He paid only for the billboard business, an *indirect* tax he could avoid by taking the billboard down.

In *Appendix C*, a deconstruction of the apparent conflict between the 1793 property rights statute and the 1875 lien statute is made, reconciling the two. Basically, the one deals with private property and the tax statute with commercial property. Yet today, the State assumes the tax statute also addresses private homes. This false authority violates three Federal criminal statutes governing the behavior of public servants (see *Hoodwinked, Volume I— Constitutional Issues* for details).

Municipal versus Commercial Corporations

Another point for the reader to contemplate is the legal status of incorporated municipalities. As one drives around, one sees markers for towns citing the town's name, indicating its date of incorporation, for example, say, in 1810.

When this incorporation took place, people in a rural district applied to the state to set up a "corporation", an entity that could conduct business in the name of those people, e.g. fix the roads. Sometimes an existing corporation already served a land area, but people in that sector wanted to break away and create their own corporation to do their bidding. State records labeled such spin-off towns as having been "taken".

Whether virgin or taken, these municipal corporations are no different from, say, "General Electric" or "McDonalds", except that GE and MD operate for the benefit of its shareholders, and the municipality for the locals. But neither municipal or commercial settings allow a corporation to bill you for things for which you did not contract them for.

Part of the illegal scam municipalities have foisted on the people includes the incorrect notion that as a by-product of incorporation, municipalities are granted special land rights to all properties inside their perimeters, rights that allow them to bill properties (under the guise of taxes) even though no agreement for the exchange of goods or services exists.

This is a false notion. Can you imagine the audacity if GE started billing people, threatening liens, where no transactions were in play?

By the way, a corollary to new municipal towns being "taken" by a new corporation, is the proposition of making one's house its own town corporation where you set the rules, and fix your own street.

Code

Speaking of tangential subjects, do you know about "administrative" code? For the longest time, I was under the delusion that our representatives in congress made our laws. Then I learned about code ... written at both State and Federal levels by "deep state" bureaucrats working either for the U.S. Presidents or the State Governors within the respective executive branches.

As background, laws passed by legislatures are typically broad-based directives that the Executive branches have a duty to implement. Regulatory departments write detailed code rules to define the enforcement specifics. The problem:

> First, these "deep state" bureaucrats write anything they want, with no requirement to check back with the legislature to ratify code details against the initial legislative decree.

> This is what Nancy Pelosi meant when she said *"We need to pass the law to see what's in it"*. ObamaCare masterminds at the White House would take care of the *"what's in it part"*, and ...

> Second, though code was started to protect *society at large* from public-impact things like improperly built skyscrapers and the need to regulate electric power, insurance, bank, pharmaceutical, and phone companies ... code somehow slipped into the domain of controlling my house (and yours).

The code bureaucrats simply manufactured home-ownership rules having nothing to do with criminal or damaging behavior, and simply put these rules into books that our local fire, building and zoning guys now use to boss people around at home. Blatantly illegal, home code violates the due process firewall keeping government away from our Life, Liberty and Property. But no one notices, and now it snowballs to authoritarian levels (One can read Hoodwinked—Volume III to see what happened to me).

So, though illegal home taxation is the focus of the three-volume **Hoodwinked** series, this runaway code situation is a sister case that the courts need to squash.

Ok, with the distinctions made between privately owned property and commercial activity, and the equivalence of municipal and commercial corporations, plus a look at "code", let's next look at what two Connecticut citizens have done about the whole property tax mess.

James Madison—Architect U.S. Constitution

Patrick Henry—Orator

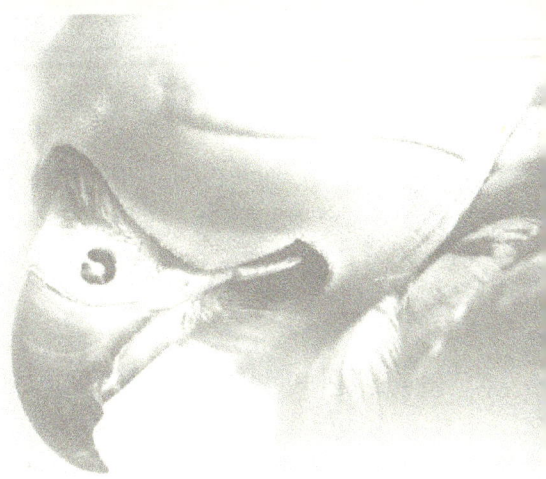

Chapter 8

Connecticut Yankees

The "twin cases" between *Patrick McCue and John Barney* (Plaintiffs filing separately) against *The Town of Simsbury,* CT (Defendant)—an attempt squashed by a local judge.

Always bear in mind that your own resolution to success is more important than any other one thing. —**Abraham Lincoln**

I mentioned Patrick McCue and John Barney earlier in this manuscript and I promised I would discuss them later in this writing. These guys actually figured out much of what I have conveyed in this document, and more so, they actually took their municipality to court—citing state-level arguments (not U.S. Constitutional arguments). As of this writing, their cases, after many years, were ultimately rejected by Connecticut's appeals court, who used explanations designed to skirt the law—as described momentarily. This chapter shows that a local challenge is futile, illustrating what happens when power players control the chess board.There were two straight-forward cases:

Case 1, "Quiet Title," asked the court to resolve who owns the property. If McCue owns his property with absolute rights, then the town cannot tax or encumber him.

Case 2, "Declaratory Judgment" asserted the tax lien—as applied to private property—unconstitutional in light of the 1793 property statute, and asks the judge to dismiss the lien.

Case 1—Quiet Title

An action to quiet title is a lawsuit brought to a judge to establish who owns title to a property. A Quiet Title suit is presented to the court against anyone and everyone, to "quiet" any challenges or claims to the title, so that the plaintive may forever be free of claims—such as taxation—against that property.

The plaintiffs simply ask the judge to affirm that as homeowners, they indeed have "Absolute and Direct Dominion and Property in the Same," the rights to property stated in CGS 47-1. After five years, no judge ruled on Case #1, allowing the town to file delaying actions.

Case 2—Declaratory Judgment

This case argues that CT 12-171-3 (12-1), the Tax Lien Statute passed in 1875—when applied to private homes—is in conflict with CT 47-1, the Connecticut Property Rights Statute passed at Connecticut's inception back in 1793, still in force today. The plaintiffs simply ask the court to order the removal of the illegal tax lien, as follows:

The property rights granted in 1793 by CT 47-1 give the titleholder *absolute* ownership over their property, with implicit protection from attached claims, liabilities, or right encumbrances that are not of ownership interest—such as taxation.

Conversely, the 12-1 Lien Statute, passed in 1875, 82 years after 1793, gives towns unchallengeable authority to encumber *commercial* property owners by placing "one-sided/non-judicial" tax liens on property.

More, the municipal corporation placing the non-judicial lien is not first required to have entered into a contractual relationship with the property holder, nor is the municipality required to have any equity interest trapped inside of the property, nor does the municipality need to conform to due process procedural rules for getting liens from court. Much of the 12-1 series is probably unconstitutional even with commercial properties, and certainly with private property.

Therefore, even with no basis or due process for a lien, municipalities use 12-1 as the authority to place a flawed lien on one's home, forcing payment of monies not owed by the property owner—in effect, a "Municipal Mafia" operation.

Case #2 had been active for years. Four out of five judges ruled in favor of McCue & Barney after the state attorney general weighed in, recognizing that based upon CGS 47-1, the state has no title claim whatsoever against the homes.

The town ignored this fact, and filed endless delaying actions holding up final judgment. Each judge accommodated the delay process, and simply let the next judge in line deal with the case's far-reaching ramifications. You may not know this, but judges have no time limit binding them to resolve a case so long as delay motions are brought forth. Collusion.

Finally, judge #5 was appointed and quickly decided to rule against the plaintiffs without even referencing statutes-in-conflict in her ruling.

An appeal petition was filed listing 16 legal infractions by the fifth judge; she really went out of her way to derail the case rather than affirm the most precious laws of the land. Her explanation "the 1875 lien statute is the most recent voice of the legislature", never segregating the fact that this voice pertained to commercial property taxation, not to private homes. Considering that the state attorney general refuses to support the lien statute when applied to homes, the judge acted brazenly for her preferred outcome—a true-blue activist judge.

Who appointed *her*?

The fix is in. The local court is dodging this straight-forward ruling.

Interestingly, both plaintiffs are self-taught regarding court proceedings (Connecticut Yankees, so to speak), representing themselves, thereby avoiding out-of-pocket expenses as the town tries to wear them down.

When parties litigate, the ability of one to wear the other down comes with the territory and is considered fair play. The difference here is that one of the parties, the municipality, is a well-funded government entity, though there are federal statutes on the books designed to protect citizens against abuse of power by government entities.

These abuse-of-power laws are titled "Color of Law" statutes, meaning the false appearance of law (i.e., fake law). The plaintiff can charge the municipality with criminal violation of these if the plaintiff can demonstrate willful abuse. Consider the Color of Law provisions below:

> "Color of Law" simply means that a person in a government official capacity, who holds the authority to implement the law, commits an illegal action under the *appearance* of authority, which exceeds such authority. Specifically, it is a violation of federal law for a lawful process to be perverted or used by a civil servant for an illicit purpose to intimidate, unduly burden, or harm another.

> In detail, a public servant violating Color of Law commits an offense if he/she intentionally subjects another to mistreatment or to arrest, detention, search, seizure, dispossession, assessment, or lien *that he/she knows is unlawful or intentionally denies or impedes* another in the exercise or enjoyment of any right, privilege, power, or immunity, knowing his/her conduct is unlawful.

In the McCue/Barney cases, the only defense the municipality and its corporate officers have is to claim ignorance of the very legal matters they have dodged for years. In the face of their long-standing exposure to the legal proceedings in play, the municipality officers need to assert a state of ignorance so unfathomable for someone to consider their behavior unintentional. The municipality knows it has no case, so it just uses its power to crush the plaintiff. This is abuse of power.

The FBI needs to take a look.

Of note: a *class action* civil case against the town is possible by home owners whose property values have been seriously lowered due to runaway property taxation. More a Nationwide class action suit by millions of willing American citizens against the states can be envisioned.

In the midst of the above, in June 2017 the court dismissed the town's request to foreclose on McCue's property. What does this mean? It meant nothing. The Town turned around and claimed it did not need judicial approval, and could take the property using a tax sale, another illicit procedure (described in detail in Hoodwinked, Volume I—Constitutional Issues).

Socialism, the Root Cause

Surely, we citizens need a legal resolution to formally repudiate property taxes as protection against town and state employees bent on collecting taxes from us.

But the real obstacle to property right justice is the built-up Socialist hold over the country. But unravelling the Socialist spider web surrounding absolute property rights presents a huge mountain to climb. Local lawyers and politically appointed judges are "little guys" tied into the system and have proven ineffective, if not corrupt.

And so, we must address this property rights conundrum at the highest levels of the U.S. Judicial System, most likely with the U.S. Supreme Court. But who can carry this water on their own? Each level of the judicial system has the perverse right to either drag out cases or refuse to hear them. Only a legal luminary with appropriate *gravitas* can cut through the spider's web. That luminary is the Department of Justice whose job it is to enforce violations of the U.S. Constitution.

To conclude this chapter, it is clear, that local judges cannot be trusted with the job at hand. Some do not want the pressure, some are socialists. One can only hope that Federal and Supreme Court appointees will relish the challenge.

Let's now look at the property rights historical progression in sequential order, seeing how the Supreme Court itself handled similar property right matters.

John Hancock—Financier

There, I guess King George will be able to read that without his spectacles! —**Hancock, upon signing the Declaration of Independence.**

Thomas Jefferson

A Bill of Rights is what the people are entitled to against every government, and what no just government should refuse, or rest on inference. — **Thomas Jefferson**

John Jay—First Chief Justice

"The law perverted, and the police powers of the state perverted along with it! Law becomes the weapon of every kind of government greed, and instead of checking crime, the law itself becomes guilty of the evils it is supposed to punish!" —**Bastiat's *The Law*, 1850**

Chapter 9

English and American Case Law

Below appears a short recap of the historical tug-of-war between Allodial and Feudal property rights, a tug-of-war that morphed into a fight between American Libertarianism and Autocratic Socialism. Let's start at the very beginning.

4,000 BC, according to the bible, God created the whole earth and gave it to all mankind—collectively: *dominion over all the earth; and over the fish of the sea, and over the fowl of the air, and over every living thing that moveth upon the earth.* In this instance, everyone took what property they needed, so long as no one else had use of it.

Back then we were wanderers, and temporary ownership was the Law of the Land. As Cicero the Roman put it: *The world was a great theater, which was common to the public, and yet the seat which any man had taken, was for the time his own.*

2,000 BC, but though the land's endless expanse was used in common, fixed possession did exist, as in the case of Abraham's water well, as explained by William Blackstone in his *Commentaries* on English Common Law, as follows:

Thus we find Abraham, who is but a sojourner, asserting his right to a well "because he had digged that well" (labor), and Isaac, ninety years later, re-claimed this his father's property (further asserting permeant possession); and after much contention with the Philistines, was suffered to enjoy it in peace.

1,000 BC, next, as mankind evolved and the population expanded, migratory living transitioned into farming, with people needing to tend the land (labor) and their livestock to survive. Fixed possession of both real property (land) and movable property (livestock) became an essential feature in the Law of the Land. Again from Blackstone's *Commentaries:*

It was clear that the earth would not produce her fruits in sufficient quantities, without the assistance of tillage: but who would be at the pains of tilling it, if another might watch an opportunity to seize upon and enjoy the product of his industry, art, and labor?

500 BC, Most societies evolved with absolute rights to property held by royal families, with feudal grants of limited rights to property sifted down the chain. It was in the Germanic world, including the Engles and Saxons of modern day Denmark, that individuals also held absolute title. The practice of having absolute title was termed "Allodial"—real property held independently of any superior landlord or chief, not encumbered by rents or taxes.

400 AD, after the fall of Rome, Anglo Saxon "freemen" invaded England, and under "common law" brought with them from Denmark, they owned land absolutely with *allodial rights*, meaning rights from God, unassailable by other men—hence the moniker "freemen." Allodial title is <u>inalienable</u> (think Jefferson), in that it cannot be taken by any <u>operation of law</u> for any reason whatsoever. Englishmen enjoyed these rights for hundreds of years, forming the bedrock of their/our "Law of the Land".

In 1066 AD, on the Hastings battlefield, the Norman French Duke *William the Conqueror* defeated *Harold Godwinson*, King of England. Under the sword, many English lords ceded their *allodial* estates to William, accepting *feudal* arrangements for these estates. With feudalism, William alone held allodial title to the estates (though some were returned), and each lord enjoyed an estate only at William's pleasure, tied to vassalage and taxation obligations.

William ruled by *Divine Right*, where a monarch is subject to no earthly authority, deriving the right to rule directly from the Will of God. The king answers not to the will of his people, the aristocracy, or any other estate of the realm—a dictator.

And so, through conquest, William obtained allodial title over many of the large English estates of the time, but notably did not obtain title to lands not yet in England's sphere, such as Scotland, Ireland, India, South Africa, Australia, or America.

In 1215 AD, to contain the dictatorial excesses of King John— an heir to William—the Magna Carta gave Englishmen the right of *due process* for government challenges against the individual, and placed limitations on feudal taxation. The King still retained allodial title to all land, and continued with the practice of allocating feudal estates to his favorites, but prosecution of subjects now followed a due process according to the "Law of the Land" designed to mitigate injustice based solely upon the whims of the monarch. People had natural rights, set above the King.

In the American era, the "Due Process Under the Law of the Land" concept was included in the 5th and the 14th amendments of the U.S. Constitution. "The Law of the Land" affirms the people's natural rights to Life, Liberty, and Property, which stand above legislative law. The government can enact no law that supersedes the natural rights of the individual. The Law of the Land is not a legislative rule or procedure; the Law of the Land is the people's born rights to Life, Liberty, and Property.

By 1300 AD, *the Writ of Replevin* came into practice in England. Replevin is an action brought by a tenant for the return of moveable property seized by the lord to satisfy a claimed debt owed to the lord. If the tenant instituted a replevin action, and gave security, the sheriff could order the lord to return the property at once, pending a final judgment in the underlying dispute. The landlord could always stop the action of replevin by proving to be the owner of the goods. Hence the process of "quiet title" begins, the need to quiet claims to title by determining the true owner. *Note: Quiet Title is one of the suits brought by McCue/Barney against the town.*

In 1620 AD, when the English colonized America, no legal authority controlled land rights in the American wilderness, and both English and Native Americans operated in a vacuum, absent of rights.

Forty years later, **in 1662 AD**, King Charles II of England, without conquest, issued land grant charters to Massachusetts, Rhode Island, and Connecticut, decreeing a system of property rights whereby one may own land in Fee Simple—Fee (ownership) Simple (minor strings attached), though the King still retained Allodial title to these lands, granting use of land under feudal decrees and minor taxation.

Before the 1776 AD American Revolution, the King asserted his allodial rights over American territories via aggressive taxation, troop quartering, and writs of assistance (random searches of property).

In this timeframe, Jefferson deconstructed the King's claim to allodial title in the Americas, pointing out that, unlike Hastings, where the English Knights ceded title to William the Conqueror, in America, no title existed anywhere and therefore title was never ceded to the King: The King's claims to title were invented and fraudulent.

In 1783 AD, following the American Revolution, England signed the Treaty of Paris, foregoing the King's claims to land inside the 13 colonies, thereby ending "invented" feudal obligations by these estates to the crown.

At the founding of The United States, our forefathers considered the right to own property a *natural right* (not one granted by government), a right possessed by all human beings, with the fundamental purpose of the Constitution to secure this natural right for all American citizens.

Property includes everything one can consider "theirs," including land, belongings, beliefs, speech, life, and liberty, and the exercise of one's intellectual faculties, with government's sole mission simply to promote a political environment where everyone could elect to make the most of their natural right to property.

Government certainly does not exist to accelerate one's right to property via handouts, or encumber one's rights to property via taxation and regulatory restrictions.

This obligation of the American government to protect the right to property—as defined in this broad sense—reaches back to old English Common Law as cited in Chapter 39 of Magna Carta, which prevents encumbrance of people and possessions without due process:

No free man shall be seized or imprisoned... or outlawed or exiled, or deprived of his standing in any other way, nor will we proceed with force against him, or send others to do so, except by the lawful judgment of his equals or by the law of the land.

In the above passage, Magna Carta compels government to follow the Law of the Land in scrutinizing any action against a citizen or the property of a citizen. The Law of the Land, protecting one's natural rights, sits above the reach of written law. Unless stated otherwise, American law first follows old English Common Law, and Magna Carta forms this Common Law basis protecting one's right to property.

In 1788 AD, the colonies ratified the U.S. Constitution. The federal government was not given any allodial rights to property within the 13 states, and reciprocally, no citizen had a feudal obligation to the federal government.

The individual states would decide upon their own property rights variations, so long as the states respected provisions in the Bill of Rights drafted upon the authority of old English Common Law, sanctifying absolute title to estates and due process.

In the U.S. Constitution, this "due process" principle is presented in the 5th Amendment, which states that:

No person can be deprived of life, liberty or property without due process of the law.

The counterforce to *Due Process* is *Police Power*, the general obligation of government to regulate citizen behavior for the safety, health, and welfare of the peoples. The 4th Amendment of the U.S. Constitution established the line not to be crossed in exercising Police Power:

The right of the people to be secure in their persons, houses, papers, and effects, against unreasonable searches and seizures, shall not be violated, and no Warrants shall issue, but upon probable cause, supported by Oath or affirmation, and particularly describing the place to be searched, and the persons or things to be seized.

In 1791 AD, Thomas Paine memorialized natural rights in his *Rights of Man* publication.

Natural rights are those which appertain to man in right of his existence. Of this kind are all the intellectual rights, or rights of the mind, and also all those rights of acting as an individual for his own comfort and happiness, which are not injurious to the natural rights of others.

In 1793 AD, Connecticut passed its land rights statute—today's CT 47-1—applicable to any fee simple landholder previously holding feudal title with the King. Thus 47-1 proclaims absolute rights and allodial title for these recent feudal land owners. Under CT 47-1, consistent with common law practices, estates can no longer be taxed or encumbered by feudal obligations.

In 1856 AD, at the onset of the Civil War, due process and property rights formed the foundation of the Republican Party's 1856 platform against the spread of slavery in the territories. The 1856 platform stated:

Our republican fathers, when they had abolished slavery in all our national territory (via the Northwest Territory Ordinance of 1787), ordained that no person should be deprived of life, liberty, or property without due process of law, it becomes our duty to maintain this provision of the constitution against attempts to violate it for the purpose of establishing slavery in any territory of the United States, by positive legislation, prohibiting its existence or extension therein...

We deny the authority of Congress, of a territory legislature, of any individual or association of individuals, to give legal existence to slavery in any territory of the United States, while the present constitution shall be maintained.

The Republican Party's predisposition to protect one's right to property stands in contrast to the Democrat Party's propensity to argue against property, looking for clever reasons to avoid the literal decrees of the Constitution. For example, the Democrat response to Republican repudiation of slavery asserts that due process refers to the slave owner, not to the slave.

This argument—blatantly ignoring every person's natural right to property and instead vesting natural rights only in some— was supported by the Supreme Court during the Dred Scott case. Regarding Scott's claim that once on "free" soil the slave became free, Justice Taney wrote:

An Act of Congress which deprives a citizen of the United States of his liberty or property, merely because... he brought his property into a particular Territory... and who committed no offense against the laws, could hardly be dignified with the name of due process of law.

In other words, Dred Scott remained a slave, even on "free" soil. Justice Tany classified Dred Scott as property not as a human with natural rights.**After the Civil War in 1865 AD Connecticut**, CT 47-1 dropped the word "allodial," but other decrees such as property rights being absolute, direct, etc., stayed put within the statute books, even to this day (Texas and Nevada still have allodial provisions).

In 1868 AD, after the Civil War, as part of an attempt to dodge due process protection by the U.S. Constitution's 5th Amendment, the Democrats put forth a cockeyed argument saying that due process—though a natural right sitting above law itself—only applied at the federal level, and that it does not obligate states for local circumstances.

To counter this absurdity, in 1868, the Republicans, who controlled Congress and two-thirds of the states, passed the 14th Amendment, clearly asserting that due process applied to all levels of American government, introducing a concept called "substantive due process" as compared to "procedural due process."

"Procedural" could mean as little as proper notices being sent to a citizen on some matter; substantive measures in the 14th amendment protect citizens from executive, judicial and majority-vote decisions that fundamentally exceed the limits of government authority. For example, a majority vote in a municipality to raise property taxes, when no tax authority exists in the first place.

The 14th Amendment re-stated hundreds of years of Common Law tradition within our Law of the Land. Due Process refers to the lawful extent of government, and not simply to procedural technicalities.

In Connecticut, in 1875 AD, the Connecticut Assembly passed its tax collection statute series CT 12-171-to-174—authorizing municipalities to lien and confiscate property to collect property taxes, without procedural due process in the courts, thereby sanctioning "non-judicial taking", an absurdity within the American system!

Tax liens created a feudal relationship between the state and the property owner, which is possible only upon contract, such as registering a business with the state. CT 47-1's design specifically prohibits such feudal coercion by the state, as does substantive due process at the federal level. Because home owners have no contracted obligations, the tax collection series cannot be applied to homes.

Appendix B will show how States incorrectly apply taxation tied to business registration to homes—forcing a feudal relationship. Only eminent domain compensation, search-and-seizure, and intestate settlement (death without a will) situations are provided for by law—obligations the state has to you, not feudal obligations one has to the state.

But by 1877 AD, anti-property forces on the Supreme Court wiggled around absolutely owned, private property. For example, in 1877, in the Munn vs. Illinois case, where

Illinois dictated the rates Munn could charge for its grain elevator services, the Supreme Court ruled against Munn in favor of Illinois:

Property becomes closed with the public interest when it is used in a manner to make it a public consequence. When one devotes his property to a use in which the public has an interest, he, in effect grants to the public an interest in that use.

Private property suddenly became public property when considered in the public's interest. This ruling, centered around economic interests, makes a key pivot from one's natural rights to property, moving down the road toward Socialism. Still, one should note, the Court never considered non-commercial private homes fair game, only commercial activity.

In the 1884 AD case of Hurtado v. California the Supreme Court stated:

Due process of law in the 14th Amendment refers to that law of the land in each state which derives its authority from the inherent and reserved powers of the state, exerted within the limits of those fundamental principles of liberty and justice which lie at the base of all our civil and political institutions.

The states cannot pass laws outside of the boundaries of the U.S. Constitution.

By 1890 AD, assuming that no crime placing someone in immediate danger is in play, government's primary authority in private homes is in eminent domain confiscation cases. Eminent domain gives the government the right to take property for some extraordinary public good, but only if the owner is fairly compensated.

For example, in the 1890's, in *United States v. Gettysburg Electric Railroad* Company, the Supreme Court ruled for fair compensation to the railroad company that owned parts of Gettysburg Battlefield when it became a National Park.

This obligation of the government to the property holder is spelled out in the 5th amendment, as follows: *"...nor shall private property be taken for public use, without just compensation."*

But in no way does eminent domain give government the right to tax the property owner; the government has obligations to pay property owners, not siphon off the owner's wealth.

Nationally, from 1877 to 1954 AD, Democrats continued to seek workarounds to everyone's natural right to property, especially with the notorious *Jim Crow Laws* passed in 1877 by southern, Democrat- controlled legislatures. Using the *separate-but-equal argument*, Jim Crow Laws finessed the assertion that all men are created equal, by asserting that one could still be separated even if equal—like chickens, all equal, placed in different coops. Protection of Life, Liberty and Property could be segregated... Socialists, controlling human life.

In 1905 AD, the Supreme Court case Lochner vs. New York limited the ability of the states to wantonly corrode the property rights of the citizens of the state. Though the forefathers designed the U.S. Constitution to leave some property law in the hands of the states, this did not mean "anything goes."

In the Lochner case, New York State passed a law butting into the private businesses of local (mainly immigrant) bakers, telling the bakers they could not work more than 10 hours per day. The law was struck down, the decision describing the attempt to limit hours not a legitimate exercise of the state's police power to protect citizens. Instead it simply encumbered immigrant bakers operating their private businesses.

Note, though, this case came out of a commercial corner; it still sided with the property owner over the police powers of the state:

The police power would serve as a mere pretext, and become another and delusive name for the supreme sovereignty of the state to be exercised free from constitutional restraint.
—**Lochner v. New York, 1905**

Again, the states cannot pass law outside the boundaries set by the Constitution.

The 1900's Due Process—In the 1900's numerous cases involving property foreclosure and due process appeared before the Supreme Court. These cases all dealt in situations with an explicit commercial agreement in place between disputing parties. In contrast, foreclosure by municipalities on homeowners where no explicit agreement exists have never been presented to the high court.

Still, the conclusions of the court in protecting individuals involved in *commercial cases* is telling, and therefore establishes a great barrier to "non-judicial takes," should citizen *private property cases* such as McCue and Barney come before the Supreme Court in future years.

Historically, within commercial cases, because of the extensive use of credit in consumer purchasing patterns, the Supreme Court confronted the problem of defining the degree of due process protection to be afforded owners of what has been called "necessary property."

Recent decisions of the Court indicate a trend toward broadening the sphere of due process protection for property interest.

In the 1969 Sniadach v. Family Finance Corporation case, Sniadach attacked the constitutionality of a Wisconsin wage garnishment procedure. A finance corporation had filed a garnishment complaint alleging indebtedness on a promissory note by Sniadach.

The garnishee employer (Sniadach's boss) answered the complaint by stating that it was in possession of wages due and that he would pay one-half of that amount to his employee, the subsistence allowance as provided by statute.

In the lower courts Sniadach unsuccessfully sought dismissal of the 50 percent garnishment action on several constitutional grounds, including deprivation of property without due process of law. It took the United States Supreme Court to reverse the decision of the lower court.

Justice Douglas, writing for the majority, stressed the fact that:

...an "interim" freezing of wages from the filing of the garnishment action to the trial on the merits was as serious as

permanent deprivation of property and "may as a practical
matter drive a wage-earning family to the wall."

The majority writing for the Supreme Court considered wages "property" needing protection under the due process clause.

The majority also expressed concern over the tendency of garnishment to deprive the defendant of a realistic judicial settlement because of the pressure on him to settle with the plaintiff and thereby pacify his employer. Here, the Court blocked *an extortion dynamic.* What would the Court think about foreclosure of one's home as a color of law extortion?

In 1972, another due process case showed the propensity of the Supreme Court regarding property protection in confiscation circumstances. In the **Fuentes v. Shevin consumer case,** Fuentes stopped sending an appliance merchant the monthly payment for a gas stove after a disagreement arose on servicing the stove.

At this point, the merchant filed an action for repossession of the stove in conformance with the Florida procedure. Before Mrs. Fuentes received notice of the action, the merchant obtained a writ of replevin directing the sheriff to seize the goods from the Fuentes' home.

Concomitant with the confiscation, the sheriff delivered notice of the underlying complaint. By virtue of the Florida statute, the petitioner received no prior notice and allowed no opportunity to challenge the issuance of the writ.

At first glance, this case appears to be about proper timing of notices, but during litigation, many property protection principles were cited that could easily apply to confiscation of one's home, and not just a gas stove. These principles included:

Substantial Deprivation—Regardless of notices, the court deemed the taking of the stove to be "substantial deprivation."

Necessary Property—The stove was "necessary property" needed to live.

Grievous Loss—Any substantial and adverse impact on one's private interests is sufficient to require due process protection. This theory provides a rationale applicable to deprivations of property. The "grievous loss" concept concentrates on the ideological protection of the individual's rights. Its application to deprivations of all types of property is apparent. How about one's home?

Overall, Fuentes and other cases show the Court's disposition to protect property at the constitutional "Due Process" level, even in commercial disputes. So far, the high court has not faced a private property case where municipal confiscation of assets takes place without even a breach of a commercial contract as the basis.

Reproductive Rights Cases

Finally, let's examine abortion case law interplay with the Constitution's Life, Liberty, and Property protections and fold the protection-of-person legacy into protection-of-the-home-owner arena.

The Abortion Cases of 1965, 1973, and 1992 offer us a peek at the sharp focus of the Supreme Court when considering the 5th and 14th Amendment due process clauses protecting Life, Liberty, and Property.

As you will see, if the courts go this far in protecting the mother's rights, even with the conundrum of a victim fetus, one can only guess the extent of court protection in defending a homeowner who simply wants to live in their home, with no victims whatsoever and no outside claims to title.

Here are the famous women's (one owns one's body) property right cases.

1965 Griswold v. Connecticut—A Connecticut statute making contraceptive drugs illegal is overturned by the Supreme Court as it violates one's right to privacy, a right inherent in the Life, Liberty, and Property clause. The use of contraceptive drugs equates to navigating one's private Liberty to best affect one's Life.

1973 Roe v. Wade—The court ruled 7-2 that a right to privacy under the due process clause of the 14th Amendment extended to a woman's decision to have an abortion. But this right needed to be balanced against the state's interests in regulating abortions: protecting women's health and protecting the potentiality of human life.

Arguing that these state interests became stronger over the course of a pregnancy, the Court resolved this by tying state regulation of abortion to the second and third trimesters of pregnancy.

The trimester aspect of this ruling gave the mother absolute rights to abortion in the first trimester, conditional rights in the second trimester tied to the mother's wellbeing, and no rights in the third trimester.

As with other property topics, the extent of absolute rights is at stake.

1992—Planned Parenthood v. Casey—The Court rejected Roe's trimester framework while still affirming Roe's central holding that a woman has a right to abortion until "fetal viability." The *Roe* decision had defined "viable" as "potentially able to live outside the mother's womb, albeit with artificial aid."

In 1992, justices in Casey acknowledged that viability may occur at 23 or 24 weeks, or sometimes even earlier, in light of medical advances.

The principle in both instances, Roe and Casey, was to award the mother with absolute rights to abortion for as much time as possible. This argument for time is made in order to protect her Liberty in affecting her wellbeing—her Life and Property—to the greatest extent possible without harming another "viable" person.

If the fetus cannot survive on its own, it is not yet a viable person due its own rights. The famous Justice Kennedy majority ruling in Casey citing Liberty as the key, follows:

> Our law affords constitutional protection to personal decisions relating to marriage, procreation, contraception, family relationships, child rearing, and education.

> These matters, involving the most intimate and personal choices a person may make in a lifetime, choices central to personal dignity and autonomy, are central to the liberty protected by the Fourteenth Amendment. And ...

> At the heart of liberty is the right to define one's own concept of existence, of meaning, of the universe, and of the mystery of human life.

All three reproductive rights cases show the extent to which the Supreme Court goes to protect a mother's Life, Liberty and Property, while factoring in the tangential rights of a living fetus. Regardless of one's personal views on abortion, the law deals strictly with one's property rights under due process, and it goes to the end of the universe to guarantee these rights.

In the case of home ownership, where there are no tangential victims with title claim to one's property, one's property rights must stay absolute at all points, regardless of the emotional desire to fund government schools by society's many pro-tax advocates. Simply put, a Socialist property tax wish agenda presented to the Supreme Court will not be authoritative up against due process any more than the anti- abortion, religious agenda was when it tried to trump due process.

Due Process versus Socialism

The 5th and 14th Amendments to the United States Constitution each contain a due process clause. Due process acts as a safeguard against the debasing of Life, Liberty, real and moveable Property by American government bodies, whereas Socialism seeks to manage the whole of society—its behavior and its property.

And so, within the American system—itself inherently anti-monarchy and anti-socialist—government at any level cannot drift outside of the Common Law and U.S. Constitutional bounds that restrict it from compromising the people's natural, absolute rights to property.

Accordingly, the Supreme Court of the United States interprets due process broadly, because these clauses provide four protections: 1.) procedural due process, 2.) substantive due process, 3.) as a vehicle for the incorporation of the Bill of Rights into our day-to-day lives, and 4.) as a prohibition against vague laws. An example of vague laws follows:

> *Legally speaking, the term 'public rights' is as vague and indefinite as are the terms 'public health,' 'public good,' 'public welfare,' and the like. It has no legal meaning.*
> — **Lysander Spooner**

Due process, therefore, ensures the minority rights of citizens against the various forms of voter, legislative, executive and judicial tyranny. It protects both the natural, absolute rights to property and the owner's liberties in disposing said property from any legal connivance that goes against the *Law of the Land.*

In America, it always comes back to property.

Under the current U.S. Constitution—the intent of which is to protect absolute rights to property as a centerpiece to America's founding—neither popular voting nor government legislation can authorize wealth taking from one's home, bank account, investment portfolio, or any other asset simply to fund municipal, state, or federal budgets.

Ask yourself, are you for or against *Natural Rights* to property?

One cannot have it both ways. Those who in the face of our Constitution rail against *absolute property rights* operate as invasive Socialists, breaking American law, making them *de facto* anti-Americans, enemies of the *Law of the Land.* If you don't want the Socialist label, then stop backing Socialist agendas and politicians. Otherwise wear a Socialist pin and be proud of it.

Socialist want the land, but not the country's philosophy. And as Margret Thatcher said, it is philosophy—the philosophy embracing Life, Liberty, and Property—that makes one an American, not the dirt one is born upon nor the place one simply immigrates to.

Accordingly, we who cherish Natural Rights want citizens and immigrants who embrace our Law of the Land. Yes, anti-American opinion is protected, but not for a minute does anti-Americanism need accommodation, allowing it to tip our Law of the Land towards dreaded Socialist ways, i.e. government control over behavior and property.

THE LAW
OF THE LAND

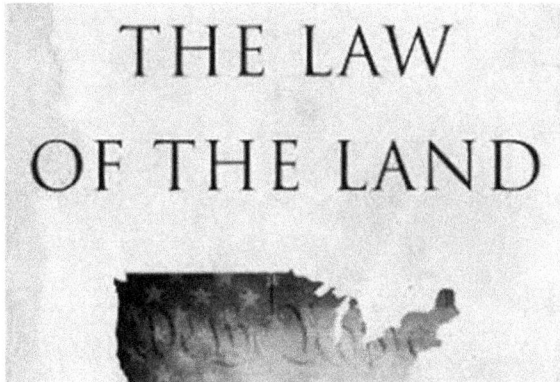

In 1855, the U.S. Supreme Court said:

The words, 'due process of law,' were undoubtedly intended to convey the same meaning as the words, 'by the law of the land,' in Magna Charta. **Murray's Lessee v. Hoboken Land and Improvement Co., <u>59 U.S. 272</u> (1855).**

Justice Curtis explained:

The article is a restraint on the legislative as well as on the executive and judicial powers of the government, and cannot be so construed as to leave congress free to make any process 'due process of law,' by its mere will.

In my words, "the government is not in charge of everything", and certainly not in charge of my house. So the question becomes: *Are we to be a nation of inalienable natural rights to property, or not?*

This land is my land. This land is your land. This land belongs to you and me.—American Folk Song. Not true ... every parcel of American land is owned by individuals, corporations, or Federal, State and Local governments. "The people" have no collective legal claim to any of it. When rangers close Yellowstone park, you must leave; it is not yours.

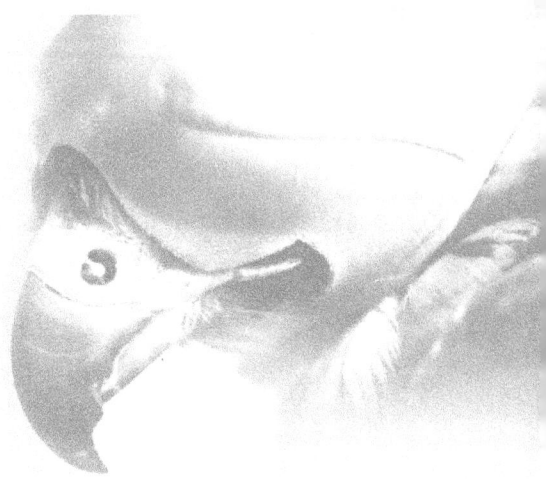

Chapter 10

Fighting for Our Law of the Land

First, A Further Word About Government Schools—by the master …

Everything has its limit—iron cannot be educated into gold.
Mark Twain

As mentioned, the 1965 Connecticut Constitution guarantees free grammar and high school educations for all, but does not attempt to pay for the benefit it bestows, leaving the towns to struggle with a veritable Gordian Knot—where is Hercules when you need him?

Not only does the "education is free" law omit funding provisions, but it does not even define education. Is education The Three R's? Does it include building artificial turf fields? Does it mean providing free lunches? Free transportation? Free computers? Cooking classes?

Does free education mean that educational institutions pick up the job of caretaking the mentally disabled? Does it mean spending any amount of money on any student for any purpose envisioned by the Board of Education or by federal "intervention" mandates?

What is this free education, anyway? The only thing not left to doubt: it's ok for someone else to pay for your kid's free education—whatever free education is.

After deciding what free education means, and because property taxes are illegal, the state can either increase its sales tax or its income tax to pay for this wonderful free education.

Sales and income taxes are the only money machine schemes the state has a legal right to power up. Then, when they pool the money, the fight begins: which schools get how much money, Greenwich versus Bridgeport, Connecticut? You see, once one embraces Socialism, it stays ugly, no matter how you try to dress it up. The only way under "equal protection" to deliver free K-to-12 education is via standard vouchers for every kid, able to be cashed in at government, private and home school education outlets. Leave our houses out of it.

Yet when focusing on town budgets and government school programs, one immediately hears: "It's not just education, someone has to pay for the roads, too." Well, in my town, the total road budget amounts to just $449 per household, and so the roads "ain't" the problem. The elephant in the room? Illegal taxation of private households to educate other people's children.

What to Do? Understand both written law and Socialist tactics, using American law to arrest Socialism's corruption of individual rights.

When stealing becomes a way of life for a group of men in a society, over the course of time they create for themselves a legal system that authorizes it and a moral code that glorifies it. —**Bastiat, The Law, 1850**

Using the government school subterfuge to tax our houses is a key aspect of the Socialist assault on traditional America. Other Socialist assault tactics are found in *The Libertarianism vs. Socialism Checklist,* coming up shortly.

Overall, Socialists endeavor to create a new Law of the Land without changing our traditions or our Constitution. Yet the United States Law of the Land still retains its roots in the historical buildup leading up to the American revolution blended with the formal constitutional protections of both the individual and one's property.

So, if we are to retain our rare liberties, we must confront Socialist maneuvering at every turn. Compromise will only work for the Socialist agenda, for with each compromise, one moves slowly away from America's Law of the Land and toward government/mob authority.

When discussing illegal taxation—just one of the tricks of Socialism—people quickly understand that both the Statutes-in-Conflict and Due Process considerations outlined herein make sense and that they inherently nullify the legal standing of municipalities to tax homeowners. But, just as quickly, they ponder the entire municipal operating model as based upon these taxes. Most conclude that homeowner taxation must unfortunately continue, and in doing so, cede their rights to Socialism.

I like to point out that by 1860, the South had built its entire economy around slavery—the very antithesis of the Constitution's Due Process protection for all people. And just as we did not permit full slavery of the person to stand then, we must not allow partial slavery of the person—through forced property taxation, liens and foreclosures—to stand now.

As Thomas Paine pointed out in his 1791 *Rights of Man*:

A greater absurdity cannot present itself to the understanding of man than that a certain body of men who existed a hundred years ago made a law, and that there does not exist in the nation, nor ever will, nor ever can, a power to alter it.

Overall, I am convinced that the top factor weakening America is the infection of property taxes across the land. Every year these taxes rob households of the wealth needed for each household's wellbeing and independence, and worse, they teach that wealth transfer is legal.

And if houses cannot be secured by due process protection, what will stop legislatures from writing laws that apply mill rates on our bank balances or our 401K values, chipping away at these as well?

Our psyches easily become accustomed to twisted rules—such as property tax and mortgage interest deductions—and like "little idiots" we run the maze, surviving by understanding and obeying—not questioning—the labyrinth of government dictates.

One day, rules for paying taxes on your checking account balance might enter H&R Block computer programs and we will accept this additional property tax as well, "'cause it's a rule…"

Clearly, America's natural and written law stand on the side of the property holder, but town, state, and federal government employees of both political parties hold the power cards, and with every breath they protect constitutional corrosion and their paychecks.

On our own, by waiting this long to push back, we individuals can no longer bring our well provisioned, massive government to heel; we have neither the money nor legal training to do so against an army of funded government attorneys. The crushing power of the government is why this book's property tax rebellion is ridiculed as "tilting at windmills."

I agree… almost. As Ayn Rand pointed out, the pyramid stands inverted; we have been subjugated—for the moment.

And so, besides ourselves, willing patriots, we need a champion, the Department of Justice, the Civil Liberties Organization, a law school leader, a Dershowitz, a private firm... someone with guts willing to fight on principle at the Supreme Court. Someone must be out there, for we are in here.

Our Unique Law of the Land

Please bear with me a moment longer as we look deeper into the power of a country's Law of the Land.

The following insights came to me during another project investigating the Mongol conquests. The Mongols prove an excellent example of how people thrive while living according to their particular Law of the Land.

Before their 100-year domination of most of the civilized world, Mongol culture already comprised warring, stealing, revenge, rape, and enslavement amongst themselves—a brutal way of life to which we cannot relate.

Hence, once Genghis Khan consolidated the tribes, turning them outward to run over entire peoples, Mongol soldiers had no psychological objections to killing every man, woman, and child they encountered, chopping off the heads to make giant piles of skulls. This did not conflict them.

None of these Mongols suffered from *post-traumatic-stress syndrome* as a result of their experiences. For good or for bad, conquest and annihilation made up part of their Law of the Land, and so they thrived in a setting that would destabilize the psychological solidity of, say, an American soldier, who believes in the natural rights of everyone.

Likewise, the Chinese, who forever lived subserviently under the emperors, came out of that ancient Law of the Land only to enter the modern Communist system, a new Law of the Land, but one that still treats individuals as drones of the hive. But being their Law of the Land, I am sure that most of the Chinese who for 5,000 years lived under these conditions thrived, living happy lives. Conforming to a pyramid of command remains the Chinese Law of the Land, not ours.

The same can be said of Russia, with its brutal czars, its brutal Communists, and now Putin, Russia's latest Totalitarian dictator. Not a single Russian commoner living in Russia has ever experienced what Americans call liberty. Life, Liberty, and Property is not Russia's Law of the Land, it's ours.

And how about India? One billion people living according to their caste at birth—racism on steroids! This is their Law of the Land, not ours.

On my honeymoon in Chile, when I thanked a local boy for lending me his guitar, the estate owners—who owned a hacienda the size of Rhode Island granted to them by Pissarro in the 1500's—pulled me aside and "educated" me that the boy cannot be treated as my equal. This is their Law of the Land, not ours. But all are happy.

And consider the world of Islam with its theocracies, Sharia Law and mutilation of woman … these are not our Laws of the Land, but theirs.

In America's case, our unique Law of the Land sits central to our happiness, more so than we realize. But due to our complacency, over the past 100 years, Socialist forces have incrementally compromised our traditions, striving for a new Law of the Land where government authority gradually trumps natural rights. The people and the people's properties are becoming subordinated. And Socialists attempt this without changing written law, by going around our legal footings. One tactic used is *illegal immigration*, as follows:

By definition, illegal immigrants are illegal, willfully violating our immigration laws and shamelessly perpetrating a massively disproportionate amount of crime. Though 7% of the population, illegals commit over 20% of the Federal crimes ... like murder, drug dealing and drug possession (U.S. Sentencing Commission, 2017). The last things many illegals are interested in are your property rights, your homes or your traditions, and hence those socialists amongst us flood America with non-Americans, to dilute the broth—importing Socialist voters and chaotic, antithetical values.

It becomes a cabal of Socialist inside of government combined with Socialist citizens and invited outside illegals, all chipping away at our Law of the Land. Traditional Americans on the Supreme Court must not give these socialist plotters any quarter whatsoever ...compromise being the socialist stealth weapon of choice against natural rights, due process, one's property, behavior and views.

Many in our society today sense this permitted incremental encroachment and it causes them chronic stress, loss of wealth and ingrained unhappiness. Yes, our American ship leans "hard to port," and our demise sickens many traditional Americans. Those on the Left live in ecstasy, hoping to reinvent a new Law of the Land subjugating what they see as "arrogant" individualism.

But we have righted the ship before. Slavery once defiled our Law of the Land in the worst possible manner, and though the Democrat South had built its entire economic world upon it, the

Republicans and Lincoln finally rooted out the institution during the Civil War.

Since then, property taxation, a new enslavement, slipped into practice. It imposed soft possession of the homeowner, as without consent or contract, municipalities began taking wealth from the individual.

Though not as grotesque as complete slavery of the whole person, home enslavement is akin nonetheless, as ultimately both deny one's right to Life, Liberty, and Property.

And as in the Old South, modern municipalities have built entire economic systems around the home enslavement practice.

I am not saying that to be an American one must be a "right wing" hater of social programs. One can tilt right or left, but if you advocate for direct interference in the lives and properties of citizens who are not criminals, then you cross the line into de facto socialism—a form of enslavement. I know of both Democrats and Republicans guilty of this. But an engrained cancer inside of our system does not make it acceptable; one can fight back. As with full slavery, it is again time to make a stand for our natural rights. The Supreme Court needs to strike down taxation of private property and put American independence back on the map. But it won't come easy.

Those who govern, having much business on their hands, do not generally like to take the trouble of considering and carrying into execution new projects. The best public measures are therefore seldom adopted from previous wisdom, but forced by the occasion. —**Benjamin Franklin**

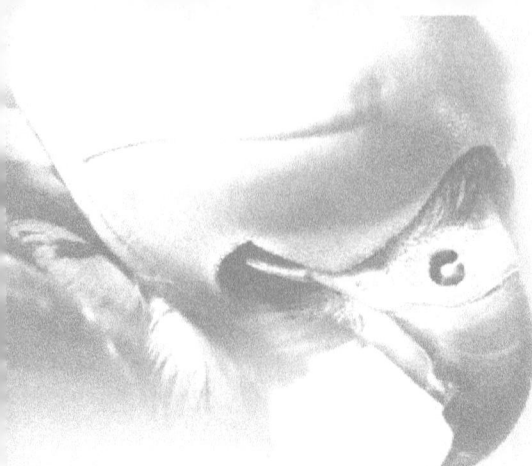

Appendix A

The Checklist

And finally, as promised, my *Libertarianism* (pro-property, pro-individual) versus *Socialism* (anti-property, anti-individual) checklist. If you are a Socialist, by this point, you are probably not reading the manuscript, as Socialists do not contemplate arguments justifying traditional American law when they solely want new *dictated* law.

Socialists actually dismiss facts, saying "I don't know about that…" or "That can't be true!" or "I don't see that", or they intentionally appear confused and hurt by your stupidity …simply pining for what they want: a managed society where we cede our inalienable, natural rights to superior government authority. Using "fair share" slogans, they harness some to open-ended tax obligations, and others to a life of dependency, controlling both halves of society. This done, they work on immigrants.

Socialist use talking points like: "Immigrants are hard-working people, doing the work we won't do; they fuel America's success, and their children are innocent", and spin like, "America is both a land of laws and a land of immigrants" … as if this false equivalency provides *carte blanch* to open the floodgates to all the earth's billions of persecuted and impoverished peoples. *America is not fueled by immigrants per se; historically, prior to welfare, America was fueled, and its early immigrants were motivated by liberty and wealth.* Today we attract different orientations. At 330 million, America has sufficient talent. Worse, one is not to call them "Socialists"; instead they condition us into using the softer "Progressive" and stolen "Liberal" monikers—wolves in sheep's clothing, insulted by the Socialist label, yet incrementing Socialism every chance they get. Go away!

John Adams, Founder

Here is the Libertarianism versus socialism checklist:

TOPIC	LIBERTARIANISM	SOCIALISM
Goal	Liberty	Obedience
Power	The Individual	The State
Decisions	By The Individual	By Pyramids of Control
Economy	Run by the Citizens	Run by the Government
Property	Strictly Private	Regulate, Tax, Confiscate
Rights	Allodial	Feudal
Wealth	Personally Earned	Owed to Society
Taxes	A Basic Contribution	Pressured Extortion
Finance	Savings	Debt
Wellbeing	Each Family's Priority	Government Promises
Government	Liberty's Protector	Wealth Transfer Agent
Military	Liberty's Protector	National Police
Congress	Our Representatives	Elite Masters
Voters	Able/The Ship's Ballast	Inferior/Need Masters
Speech	Unfettered	Muzzled
Debate	Encouraged	Distract People with It
Education	Knowledge/Critical Thinking	Crafted Indoctrination
Teachers	Encyclopedias	A Union Voting Block
Electorate	Expect Honesty	Stupid, Lied To, Duped
Press	Independent/The Facts	An Ally/A Spin Department
Immigration	A Trickle, Vetted	A Flood, Illegal
Religion	Accepted	Shunned
Environment	Preservation	Political Opportunity
Guns	Right to Self Defense	A Disarmed Citizenry
Race	Irrelevant	Victims, A Divider
Sexuality	Irrelevant	Victims. A Divider
Opportunity	Educate, Train, Intern	Spread Dependency
America	Blessed/Extraordinary	Change It, Socialize It, End It

Socialism—Government control over property, economy, behavior and views—runs illegal in the American system. You can vote for Socialism, *but you cannot legally use people's property to advance and pay for your agendas.*

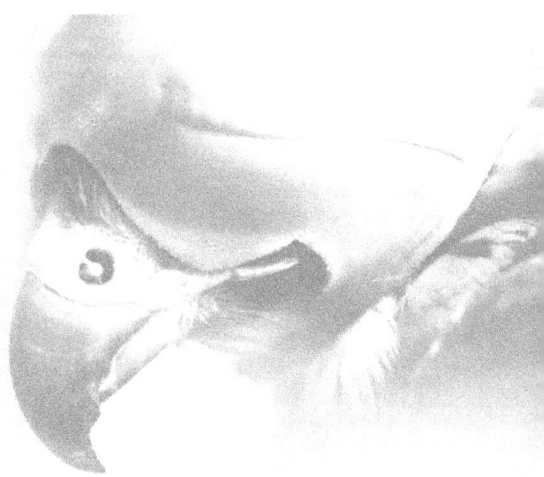

Appendix B

Natural Rights

The sacred rights of mankind are not to be rummaged for among old parchments or musty records. They are written, as with a sunbeam, in the whole volume of human nature, by the hand of the divinity itself; and can never be erased. — **Hamilton, The Federalist Papers** author wanting America's Law of the Land to sit above government authority.

Hamilton

A man's natural rights are his own, against the whole world; and any infringement of them is equally a crime, whether committed by one man, or by millions calling themselves a government. —**Lysander Spooner, 1845, The Unconstitutionality of Slavery**.

Jefferson

I close with Jefferson; I guess he was the smartest guy in the room. Please listen.

The democracy will cease to exist when you take away from those willing to work and give to those who would not.

It is incumbent on every generation to pay its debts as it goes.

I predict future happiness for Americans if they can prevent the government from wasting the labors of the people under the pretense of taking care of them.

Experience hath shewn, that even under the best forms of government those entrusted with power have, in time, and by slow operations, perverted it into tyranny.

Whenever the people are well-informed, they can be trusted with their own government.

The strongest reason for the people to retain the right to keep and bear arms is, as a last resort, is to protect themselves from tyranny of government.

To consider the judges as the ultimate arbiters of all constitutional questions is a very dangerous doctrine indeed, and one which would place us under the despotism of an oligarchy.

We hold these truths to be self-evident, that all men are created equal; that they are endowed by their Creator with certain inalienable rights; that among these are life, liberty, and the pursuit of happiness.

Jefferson

Appendix C

Indirect and Direct Taxation & Apportionment

The U.S. Constitution makes the distinction between indirect and direct taxes. Let's start with **indirect commercial taxation** (taxes owed for doing)—meaning that a commercial transaction has taken place where cash is exchanged for goods, services, homes, interest earned, dividends due, employment rewarded or rent owed. All of these moving targets are taxed, so long as you participate in the economy. For example:

Sales Tax—Indirect, where the buyer has some control over their buying activities (hence an indirect tax). By buying cheaper wine, and one pays less tax.

Conveyance Tax—In places like New York City, the seller pays the city for the right to buy an apartment. Indirect, as not forced to buy.

Income Tax—Indirect, don't work so hard, where one pays a percent of one's income …unheard of until the 16th Amendment was ratified in 1913.

Investment Income—Indirect, don't risk investment. Other than right-offs for expenses and losses (for now), any government authority can collect a percentage of one's interest, dividend, capital gain or rental income receipts.

Fee Taxes—Indirect, where one has marginal control, such as with car registration fees. Marginal, as who can risk not registering and paying the DMV when the police will tow your car and possibly handcuff you for skipping the process? BTW, Connecticut's governor wanted a fee for getting a haircut, but was talked out of it!

Now let's look at **direct property taxation** (taxes owed simply for living, dying and owning things), all direct in nature, but simultaneously all illegal, as Natural Rights and Due Process shield our Life, Liberty and Property from such government moves. Here are the Direct categories.

Poll Taxation—Direct, without choice, where each person pays the government for being alive (done in England, and implemented briefly in America—slaves were charged 3/5$^{ths)}$. Poll taxes—for being alive—are easily resented. In 1381, when English tax collectors tried, for the third time in four years, to levy a Poll Tax, it caused "the peasant's revolt". With the war against France going badly, and the government's reputation already damaged, the tax due *for being alive* was 'the last straw'.

Death Taxes, due *for dying*, are direct, without real choice—unless one cedes assets to charities. This tax has been claimed, so far, by both State and Federal entities against the families of dead people. Municipalities might just as well jump in and get a cut, as they already have no care for our Natural Rights to Life, Liberty and Property. If municipalities can take the living person's home, why not double up and take a dead person's home? (Think of Isaac claiming ownership of his father Abraham's well. Even the Philistines—of Goliath fame—did not take the desert well upon Abraham's death).

Real Estate Taxation—Direct, without choice, due *for owning a house*, pursued in history by Federal, State and Local governing entities, though today, only municipalities extract monies using this claim. Historically, the Federal government *illegally* imposed property taxes after the Revolution, the War of 1812 and the Civil War, but never tried it again (cross your fingers).

Financial Assets—Direct, without choice, due for *owning anything*, things like checking and brokerage accounts, 401 K's. So far these personal balances are not taxed in America, but there is nothing (other than Natural Law, Due Process and Self Defense) from stopping socialist politicians from grabbing this ultimate prize. Recently in Cyprus, the government there needed cash, and it took a percentage of every account at every bank in the country.

Article I, Section 2 of the Constitution *states* that direct taxes be apportioned pro rata among the states by population. That is why, in 1913, the Income Tax Amendment was engineered to specifically give government the right to use *non-apportioned formulas* in concocting *income tax* schemes. No such exception to apportionment was ever made for *property*. More, no direct property taxes have been sanctioned by the Supreme Court since the passing of the *substantive due process* clause of the 14th Amendment in 1868. I sense that through *Substantive Due Process,* Congress finally concluded direct taxation never to be a legal option again. Should apportioned property taxation be merited, it would look like this ...

Have state revenues pay for state mandates such as free K-to-12 education, building and fire code administration. Divide the remaining town budget covering police and roads by resident adults, with each paying a proportionate "poll" share, and watch the budget evaporate! Cannot pay? Foreclosure, removal and loss of residency—just like now.

The *Separatist Puritans* knew their Law of the Land would be siphoned off by impractical *Vanilla Puritan* agendas, and hence they stayed separated. Today, Socialists live amongst us, with physical separation not practical, and so, short of armed conflict, separation via *due process* remains the only option for preserving pro-individual and pro-property *Americanism*. *Hoodwinked* encourages the higher courts to respect this by eliminating direct home taxation. Doing so will once more re-assert our natural rights to Life, Liberty and Property. For details, see *Hoodwinked, Volume I—Constitutional Issues.*

Appendix D

Socialist Engineering of Society

Finally, in case you feel I exaggerate regarding the intent of socialism, please consider the following.

The theory of Communism may be summed up in one sentence: Abolish all private property.—**Karl Marx**

* * *

Give us the child for 8 years and it will be a Bolshevik forever.—**Vladimir Lenin**

* * *

We would not let our enemies have guns, why should we let them have ideas.—**Joseph Stalin**

* * *

Socialism, reduced to its simplest expression, means the complete discarding of private property transforming it into public property.—**George Bernard Shaw**

* * *

If you were successful, somebody along the line gave you some help... Somebody helped to create this unbelievable American system that we have that allowed you to thrive. Somebody invested in roads and bridges. If you've got a business—you didn't build that. Somebody else made that happen.—**Barack Obama**

* * *

We're going to take things away from you on behalf of the common good.—**Hillary Clinton**

* * *

I am a socialist, and everyone knows it.—**Bernie Sanders**

* * *

There is nobody in this country who got rich on their own—nobody.—**Elizabeth Warren**

* * *

Healthcare as a human right, it means that every child, no matter where you are born, should have access to a college or trade-school education if they so choose it, and I think no person should be homeless if we can have public structures and public policy to allow for people to have homes and food and lead a dignified life in the United States. .— **Alexandria Ocasio-Cortez**

Don't help these people.

www.ingramcontent.com/pod-product-compliance
Lightning Source LLC
Chambersburg PA
CBHW030252030426
42336CB00009B/349